Dieter Graf

Santoríni Sífnos Kea

Western & Southern

Cyclades

Anáfi
Folégandros
Ios
Kéa
Kímolos
Kíthnos
Mílos
Santoríni
Sérifos
Sífnos
Síkinos

Hiking and Swimming for Island-Hoppers
50 walks on 11 Greek Islands

Graf Editions

Using this illustrated walking guide

AWT stands for Actual Walking Time – excluding any breaks! The AWT serves as a personal control as to whether certain route sections, emphasised in **bold print,** have been reached roughly within the given time.
The approximate **overall length** of a walk is about twice as long as the AWT and is specified in hours in the introduction to each tour. These figures do not include time taken for bus trips or extra-long breaks. Information concerning the **length of the walks,** the **difference in altitude (elevation gain)** and the **three levels of difficulty** can also be found.
Route photos are intended for orientation, for consulting locals and as a stimulus. The corresponding text is marked by [1] to [4].
The **route sketches** have been drawn to the best of our knowledge but lay no claim to completeness.
GPS points are shown as **P** in texts and on maps. Map datum WGS 84.
We would be grateful for useful information concerning changes in paths and similar data. As a token of our appreciation we will send you a free copy of our next edition. The website www.graf-editions.de informs you of changes that occur along walking routes.

The author Dieter Graf is an architect who has travelled all over the world. He has walked the Aegean Islands since the years when tourism was just beginning there and is considered a connoisseur of the islands.

Edition Dieter Graf, Elisabethstr. 29, 80796 Muenchen
www.graf-editions.de

Type-Setting: Michael Henn, Hersbruck · Maps: Kurt Zucher, Markt Indersdorf
Translation: Myles Oliver, Muenchen

Original Title: "Wandern auf Griechischen Inseln: Santorin, Sifnos, Kea, Westliche und Suedliche Kykladen" (ISBN 978-3-9814047-8-4)

Cover Photo: Sifnos, Chryssopigí peninsula (14)

ISBN 978-3-9814047-9-1

Contents

The Western and Southern Cyclades

Cyclades – sparkling sea, cube-shaped houses, gnarled olive trees, brilliant light ...
The first to succumb to this magic were the rucksack tourists of the 1970s. They loved the individual travelling through the islands, the simple life, the typical cuisine, the freedom.
That all still exists today. In the search for cheap and safe travel destinations Greece has been growing in popularity for years. Not only among individual travellers who drift from island to island, but also families with children are thrilled about the Greek islands because of the endless possibilities they offer. Away from the mass tourism it is possible to find accommodation of every standard, but no giant hotels. And cosy tavernas which serve up traditional dishes.
The name Cyclades derives from the Old Greek word *Kýklos,* meaning "circle". The way the Ancient Greeks saw it, the islands are grouped around the holy island of Délos in the form of a circle. The western and southern Cyclades described in this book embrace such differing islands as the chic Santoríni, the sleepy Sífnos and the one which is hardly noticed by foreigners, Kéa.
The Cyclades are characterised by a wide open and tranquil landscape. The endless sea can be seen from almost everywhere. Wherever he goes, the hiker captures the scents of herbs and spices. In the villages it is still possible to experience the Filoxénia, or hospitality which almost makes one forget that one is a foreigner.
To get to know the islands properly, it is necessary to walk across them. Many of the old wall-lined mule tracks still link the towns and often abandoned monasteries. But equally one can discover paths to hidden rocky bays. With hardly any fences, one is free to roam more or less where one pleases.
Each island has its specific charm; particularly suitable for hiking are Sífnos and Kéa, perhaps followed by Síkinos and Sérifos. Every reader will decide for himself; sooner or later everyone will find "his" island.

April 2016 Dieter Graf

Have a good trip *Kaló taxídi*!

Walking the Cyclades

The islands of the Cyclades rank among the finest hiking regions in Europe. The landscape is still criss-crossed by many **paved and wall-lined paths.** For centuries the narrow *monopátia* used to help the farmers work the fields and, up until 30 years ago, formed a dense network of tracks. By contrast, the up to four metre wide paved tracks, the *kalderímia,* connected larger villages for the transport of goods and served as paths for pilgrims to the monasteries. Often they were paved with marble. Some of them are said to be up to 1000 years old.

Motorisation has not failed to leave its mark on the islands either. Instead of mules the farmers now mostly use pickups, which require wider roadways. The old network of tracks was torn apart by broadening the mule tracks to make them accessible to cars wherever it seemed to be necessary and by pushing aside the dry walls along the waysides, all co-financed by money from the European Union Regional Funds. The remaining paths are now superfluous and neglected and are gradually being forgotten by the islanders. Now, however, the EU Leader Fund provides money to restore some of the remaining mule tracks, mainly for the sake of tourism. And the local councils on the islands, too, have come to realise that hiking enjoys great popularity among the guests and therefore expanded the tourist attractions. Recently almost every island has cleared paths and had them marked. Most have been mapped as well. The extent of the ongoing maintenance does vary, though. After the winter rains paths, if they have scarcely been used, are often overgrown and need to be cleaned. This book aims to help ensure that the old mule tracks which still exist are used again and hence preserved before they are irreparably destroyed.

The routes described have been walked along again shortly before publication and can be followed without difficulty by people in normal physical condition. Most of the walks are suitable for children. Special surefootedness is not necessary. Featured at the end of the book is a **diagrammatic overview** to help select the most suitable ones. The ↙ markings in the text concern only those who are very afraid of heights. For longer walking tours **short cuts** are indicated. Due to the good views, the tours normally lead from the mountains to the sea – so take along your swimming gear. You should be absolutely sure to pick a nice day for tours in the mountains since there is always the danger of sudden fog formation. Moreover it can rain there even in summer. On the other hand there is a risk of bush and forest fires in the summer.

If you want to walk alone, for **emergencies** you should by all means leave information in your hotel and save the number of the hotel on your mobile phone. As the emergency number Greece has also introduced (0030) 112. The firemen know their way about the terrain very well and are able to assist.

In order to get your blood circulation going, you should begin leisurely for the first fifteen minutes and, during the tour, **eat and especially drink often**, even if you don't feel the need to do so. The route maps show springs and wells to be found by the wayside. Be sure to protect yourself sufficiently against sun and wind too.

Coloured dots and arrows can often be found as **markings along paths**, but they do not necessarily correspond to the descriptions in this book. In addition there are the wooden signs and little red-and-white metal signs of the Greek organisations. Lately good **trail maps** have started appearing in the bookshops, for example from the Greek publishers Anavasi, Skaï-Terrain and Nakas-Road. These partly vary in quality though. But sometimes the maps show paths which can scarcely be made out on site. The maps can also be bought outside Greece.

As new roadways continue to be built, it may be that the route descriptions are partly out of date, thus calling for certain **orientation skills.** If you have orientation problems, you should always ask the locals about the "monopáti", otherwise you will be directed to roads for vehicular traffic. Mule dung on the narrow paths is more certain to lead you further than goat droppings since the goat paths usually end somewhere in the scrub, while mules always return to their stalls. If you lose your way, you may have to shin up a field wall or climb over steel mesh used as grazing fences with the help of a pile of stones. Pasture fences are knotted shut on the side where there are two perpendicular rods. You owe it to the farmers whose land you walk across to shut the openings again afterwards, of course. Access to the sea is allowed in Greece as a matter of principle.

Almost all the starting and finishing points are served by **public buses,** even in the low season. In case a service does not operate, take a taxi. A possibility for circular walking tours is a relatively reasonable rental car or a rental motor bike. In addition, car drivers also enjoy taking along a wanderer who waves them down.

Appropriate **hiking gear** includes a backpack for a day, shoes with good soles (no sandals), comfortable socks, long trousers or zipper trousers*, a mobile phone, binoculars, a whistle, a small flashlight and picnic equipment. In the spring and autumn, rainwear is a necessity. A GPS device or a compass would also be good, but is not necessary if you have a fairly good sense of orientation.

*The legs of zipper trousers which also have vertical zippers can be zipped together to form a pad to sit on at the beach. And if you connect both zippers, you have a chic skirt for visiting monasteries.

Climate and Walking Seasons

The typical temperate Mediterranean climate with a hot summer and a mild rainy winter predominates on the Cyclades. The maximum **air temperature** is 32° C in August (at night 22° C). In winter the temperature sinks to 15° C (7° C) in February. On mountains above 1000m snow can fall every 3–4 years and even lie for a short while.

The **water temperatures** are lowest in February at 16° C and reach an almost subtropical 25° C in August. You can go swimming from the end of May at 19° C through to October (22° C).

The **rainy days** are spread irregularly throughout the year. Most of the rain falls in December and January, when it rains on about 14 days. You must still calculate with 3 days of rain in May, while there is absolute dryness from June to August. Statistically October again has 6 days of rain, but it is not very plentiful.

The number of **hours of sunshine** per day corresponds to this pattern. In December and January the very strong winter sun only shines for about 4.5 hours. Even in May the wanderer must reconcile himself to 10.1 hours of sunshine per day and the swimmer to 12.1 in August. October is once again pleasant for autumn walkers, with 7.8 hours of sunshine per day.

Strong **north winds** are characteristic of the Aegean Islands, with three to four Beaufort on a yearly average. One reason for this is the difference in air pressure between the Azore highs and the hot low pressure areas above the Persian Gulf. In the transition season, especially in April and May and then October and November, the *Boréas* dominates, a cool, wet north wind. In the summer (May to September) the famous etesien winds, called the *meltémia,* often blow for days under a cloudless blue sky, regularly strong from north to northeast, with velocities of five to six Beaufort. The sky can then be somewhat overcast. Towards evening the meltémi usually slackens somewhat, but it can also blow with considerable strength for days on end.

The *sirocco* occurs less frequently, but especially in spring. It comes from the hot Sahara desert, picking up moisture over the Mediterranean to bring the Aegean warm humidity from the south.

On the Greek islands there are several different **seasons for walking** tours. Anyone wishing to feast his eyes should plan his tour around Easter. It might be somewhat cool and even muddy, but the countryside is grass-green, poppy-red and broom-yellow; the houses and alleyways are freshly whitewashed. The preparations for the Greek Easter celebration alone make the trip worthwhile. However, you can't go swimming yet, and some hotels and tavernas are still closed. In April it can rain briefly. The Greeks divide the year into three parts, and this one is called "the time of blossoming and maturing".

In May and June the blossom time is already partially over, but, since it is very warm and the number of tourists is still limited, this is probably the most attractive time for walking. Beginning at the end of May the water has a pleasant temperature.

The main tourist season in July and August is not highly recommended for walking tours due to the heat. It is the "dry period" in Greece. The dry north winds, which blow continuously, still make the temperatures bearable, but at noon it is wise to seek a shady spot under a tree. Harvest time begins in July. On 15th August, the Assumption of the Virgin, called "Passing Away Peacefully" in the Eastern Church, there are great celebrations everywhere with roast lamb, music and dance.

From the beginning of September on, the heat is over and the sea still has a pleasant temperature for swimming, up until the end of October. Now it is again possible to take longer walking tours, but only until about 6 pm due to the shorter period of daylight. The land has become yellow and brown, the fields bear their fruit, and everywhere you meet friendly farmers harvesting their last crops. From the beginning of October on, it can start to rain again. The restaurants and hotels gradually shut down and some owners travel to their winter residences in Athens. Others put on camouflage suits, reach for their guns and search through the undergrowth. A million Greeks are passionate hunters. In November there is usually a change in climate, with heavy rainfall. Then it becomes unpleasant. The period from November to February is called the "rain season". Although there are some warm, sunny days around Christmas, it is more pleasant at home.

Geology

The northern Aegean was not flooded by the sea until after the last ice age. Up until then the present island arc between Crete and Rhodes formed the southern edge of the mainland.
The more northern Cycladic islands stand on a submarine mountain which was raised out of the sea 50 million years ago by the pressure of the African continental plate on the European continental plate. After repeated rising and subsiding the islands assumed their current form. That is why one encounters slate, a sedimentary rock which was lifted out of the sea and sits on top of a bed of marble and granite. If the pressure exerted on the European continental plate persists, this will ultimately lead to the islands being lifted further out of the sea and, after about 50 million years, the Mediterranean sea disappearing altogether. Then there will be a land connection between Africa, Asia and Europe.
On the southern edge of the Aegean an active seismic arc extends from the Peleponnesus via the islands Póros, Mílos, Santoríni, Anáfi, Níssiros and Kos as far as the Taurus mountain range in Turkey. The pressure created by the land masses discharges itself here now and again as earthquakes. Half the earthquakes in Europe occur in Greece, which in addition has dormant, but also active volcanoes such as on Mílos and above all on Santoríni. These southern islands consist of volcanic tuff and lava resting on older, non-volcanic rocks.

Fauna

As a result of the mostly low vegetation large game is not encountered. The animals one most often comes across are goats and sheep, though not in such large numbers as in former years. Hares and martens are rare.
Along the way you frequently see the small common lizard, which can be up to 10 cm long. The dragon-like agama (hardun) [1], its bigger relative, is up to 30 cm long.
The careful wanderer will rarely see snakes. There is only one poisonous type: the horn or sand viper (vipera ammodytes meridionalis) [2]. It can be up to 50 cm long and as thick as two thumbs. A healthy adult hardly need fear a deadly bite.
The non-poisonous sand-boa is about the same size; it lives in very concealed spots. The non-poisonous four-striped-adder reaches an adult length of more than a metre and a width al-

most as thick as an arm. Its size is frightening, but it is harmless, as is the ring-snake.
Scorpions reaching a size of up to 5 cm also live here. A bite is rather painful but not perilous. They love to hide in shoes.
You can rouse crabs, frogs, eels and water turtles along the watercourses. In rocky bays you can sometimes discover sea urchins [3], but keep well clear of them. Monk seals live on the island of Poliégos near Mílos.

Flora

Along with Spain, Greece has the greatest variety of plants in Europe. Nevertheless, ever since antiquity forests on the Aegean islands have been cut down for building ships or have become victims of forest fires in summer, causing some parts of the countryside to seem like karstland. This effect is intensified by the limestone soil which cannot store water.
The **stock of trees** consists mainly of aleppo pines [1], from which the resin for retsina wine is obtained. Taller evergreen

4

5

6

oaks and kermes oaks [2] grow in protected regions which are rich in water. Unassuming, salt-tolerant tamarisks [3] are found along beaches. Plane-trees [4] shade the village squares and slender cypresses the cemeteries. Acacias, poplars, alders, maples and eucalyptus trees [5] can also be found, as well as mulberry trees [6] and carobs [7]. Among the fruit trees there are pomegranates, fig trees [8] and citrus fruits. Yet dominating the landscape most of all is the olive tree, which looks strangely deformed as it gets older.
On slopes and mountain tops, dry shrubs reaching a height of up to half a metre predominate, thorny undergrowth called **phrýgana** in Greek. Typical representatives of this "low macchia" are broom, thorny knap-weed (centauria spinosa), heather, spiny spurge plants (euphorbia) [9] [10], plants often shaped like hedgehogs.
Thicker bush or tree groups up to two metres high with evergreens and bushes with hard leaves are not found as frequently. This "high macchia" is called xerovumi in Greek. Kermes oaks with serrated leaves [2], juniper and mastic bushes [11] are particu-

7

8

9

larly predominant. Mastic bushes are used for manufacturing rubber and raki spirits.

The keeping of goats has caused the beginnings of higher vegetation to be kept low. Sometimes even grazing land is burned in order to give the goats the freshly growing sprouts as food. Inedible plants such as Jerusalem sage, squill or asphodel [12] grow here quickly.

Agaves (agave americana) [13] often line the lanes and paths. This thorny leaf plant has only grown in the Mediterranean area since the 16th century. Fig-cactus [14], with its thorny but tasty fruit, is also widespread.

A surprisingly abundant splendour of **flowers** appears in the spring. Already in January the anemone and crocus blossom. From February to April white and red blossoming rockroses [15], iris, yellow daffodils, hyacinths, lupines, chrysanthemums and broom add magic to the landscape with their cheery colours, and the poppy adds its bright red.

Small **orchids** are an adornment of spring for a short time. The bee orchid (ophrys) [16], lax-flowered orchid (orchis), tongue or-

chid (serapias) and dragon arum 17 can be seen frequently.
In May and June the main blossoming season comes to an end, but summer doesn't mean brown wilderness by any means. Bougainvillea radiates its bright colours on the house walls, and oleander blossoms in moist spots. The thorny acanthus 18 and the gold thistle 19 bloom along the wayside.
In the late summer and autumn the flora begins to come alive again and blossom after the first brief rain showers. Meadow-saffron, heather and squill reveal themselves along with the crocus-like stellaria bergia, dandelions, thistles and cyclamen.
Many of the plants contain ethereal oils. In the heat of the day you can especially appreciate the pleasantly spicy aroma of thyme, rosemary, lavender, oregano, camomile and fennel. Sage 20, capers 21 and other kitchen herbs often border the walking paths.

A brief history

The Cyclades have been settled since the Mesolithic period (7500 BC). Traces of settlements dating back to the end of the 4th millennium BC have been proven at Korissía on Kéa and on the small island of Sáliegos near Páros. This is when the obsidian export from Mílos begins, the hard black volcanic rock. The islands' position between Europe and Asia makes them a bridge between the cultures and one of the oldest landscapes in Europe to be cultivated very early.
During the transition from the Stone Age to the Bronze Age Europe experiences its first artistic climax, the **Cycladic culture** (3200-1100 BC). The flat female figures with folded arms made of marble are famous. The creators of these up to 1.50 m high idols strongly influenced Mycenaean art.
Four thousand years ago the Phoenicians arrive from the coast of what is now Lebanon. They impart the skills of the Assyrians and Babylonians to the Greeks, as well as introducing writing and money. Then the islands come under the influence of Minoan Crete, which establishes settlements on Santoríni and Mílos. Around 1650 BC the volcanic eruption on Santoríni destroys much of what man has so far created.
Following the decline of Crete around 1450 BC Mycenaean settlers from the Peleponnesus land and dictate subsequent events. On the mainland the Indo-European Dorians immigrating from the north later trigger a migration of peoples. After 1100 BC the islands of the Aegean and Asia Minor are colonized from there in several waves. The northern Cyclades are dominated by the Ionians, while the southern islands are later ruled by the spartan Dorians.

Archaic Period (800–500 v. Chr.) The Ionians are the first to release the Greek spirit in the sense of artistic, intellectual and economic freedom. In the sixth century BC the leadership of Greek culture is found on the islands. The mainland does not adopt these ideas until later. In terms of architecture it seems that stone temples were built on the islands much earlier.
Starting in 540 BC, the Persian Empire extends its influence to the coast of Asia Minor. Athens takes a stand and makes Délos the intellectual and cultural centre of the Attic-Delian maritime alliance. This protective league against Persia unites the Greeks in the Aegean and Asia Minor with Athens. War is unavoidable and begins in 490 BC.

The Classical Period (490–338 BC) Some Dorian islands fight on the side of the enemy at the beginning of the Persian Wars, but they, too, are on Athens' side for the final triumph over the Persians in 449 BC. Immense riches are amassed on Délos during the "Golden Age" which follows. When Athens carries off the treasure and tries to make vassals of its allies, the latter fight against Athens in allegiance to Sparta in the Peloponnesian War, that lasts 30 years. The outcome is a forever weakened Greece.

Hellenistic Period (338–146 BC) The Macedonians in northern Greece take over Greek culture after conquering Greece in 338 BC. For a short period Alexander the Great, a Macedonian, takes this culture, henceforth known as "Hellenism", as far as India. After his early death his world empire rapidly disintegrates into Ddiadochean empires, the Aegean islands being dominated by the Egyptian Ptolemies.

Roman Period (146 BC – 395 AD) After 146 BC the Romans, as the next rulers, also make Greek culture their own, thus helping it to spread throughout Europe. Greek culture becomes that of the Occident. From Rome comes Christianity, which also becomes the state religion in the Eastern Roman Empire after 391. Already before that there were Christian communities hidden away, for example on Mílos.

The Byzantine Period (395–1204 AD) The Roman Empire is divided in 395 AD. While the Western Roman Empire is in decline after the migration of peoples in 476 AD, the eastern part of the Imperium Romanum remains an upholder of Graeco-Roman culture for 1000 years. Byzantium, the second Rome, turns eastwards, brings Christianity to the Slavs and spreads Greek ideas as far as Moscow, which later becomes known as the Second Byzantium or Third Rome. The new Islamic ideas also influence Greece in the 8th and 9th centuries. The iconoclastic controversy revolves around the admissibility of a pictorial representation of God and the Saints. The image worshipers prevail.
Europe begins to drift apart in cultural terms; the religious differences also deepen. The main points of dispute concern the Holy Ghost and the corporeal ascension of Mary. In 1054 the schism, or final separation of the Eastern Greek-Orthodox Church from the Western Latin Church, comes about.
In these uncertain times the islands of the Aegean are often attacked by raiders such as the Vandals, the Goths, the Normans

and finally the Saracens. The inhabitants of the islands withdraw into the mountain villages. It isn't until the 9th century that Byzantium can consolidate its power once again.
Now, however, in the wake of the Persians, Avars and Arabs, a new Asian power has assembled on the eastern borders of Byzantium: the Turkish Seljuks. They push westward with immense force. In 1095 the Eastern Roman Empire requests help from Pope Urban II, and the crusades begin. They are a fiasco. During the fourth crusade one of the most short-sighted campaigns in history is initiated. Due to trade rivalries Venice induces the crusaders to plunder and occupy the Byzantine capital, Constantinople, in 1204. The quadriga on San Marco square is part of the loot. Not until 1261 do the Byzantians conquer the city again with the aid of the Genoans, thus terminating the Venetians' "Latin Empire". Byzantium is too weak to ever recover again and is conquered by the Turks in 1453.

The Era of the Knights (1204–1537) For most of the islands Venetian domination begins after the sack of Constantinople. They are handed over to the influential Venetian families as fiefs. For 600 years foreign rulers now set the agenda – perhaps one of the reasons for the Greeks' still perceptible disaffection with the state.
But the Turkish-Ottoman Empire directs all its energy towards conquering Europe. After the fall of Rhodes, the strongest fortress of Christianity, in 1523, the Turks push on further west. In 1537 they conquer all the Cycladic islands apart from Tínos.

The Turkish Era (1537–1830) After the Fall of Constantinople learned Byzantine fugitives bring the Greek way of thinking back to the West again, paving the way for the Renaissance. From this time on the fortune of the Orthodox Church is determined in Moscow, which assumes the Byzantine double-headed eagle as its state coat of arms.
Yet in Greece itself the Turkish influence, from diet to music, predominates for the next 350 years. This influence is still discernible today.The Orthodox Church is recognised by the Turks as a mediator between government and population and proves to be the protector of Greek culture during this period.
Russian Pan-Slavism under Catherine the Great seeks to release the Balkan Slavs from the Turkish sphere and bring them into the Russian fold. The Turkish-Russian war of 1768 to 1774 extends as far as the Aegean, where a Russian fleet occupies 18 Cy-

cladic islands for four years; they later return to Turkish rule.

Independent Greece (since 1821) In 1821 the insurrection against the Turks begins on the Peloponnesus as Turkey has been weakened after another war against Russia. Europe reflects on its cultural roots. The political stability of post-Napoleonic Europe and Classicism in art increase an awareness of eastern Europe. Philhellenists from many countries support the Greek struggle for independence, the Great Powers in Europe help diplomatically, and Greece becomes part of Europe again.
At the beginning of the twentieth Century Greece tries to regain possession of its former settlements in Asia Minor from the "sick man on the Bosporus". After the First World War, among whose losers is Turkey, the opportunity appears favourable. The Greeks start a war over the former areas. But Turkey, emboldened once again by the "Young Turk Revolution", utterly destroys the Greeks, who then have to agree to a major population exchange. In 1940 fascist Italy vainly attempts to occupy the country, whereupon German troops advance across the Balkans to Greece. They hand the country over to the Italians as occupied territory, but then occupy it themselves after Mussolini's fall in 1943, remaining on some islands until the end of the war.

After World War II With Western help during the civil war from 1945 to 1949, Greece avoids the fate of the other Balkan countries, and doesn't disappear behind the Iron Curtain. After admission to the European Union, the latter's subsidies serve to improve the infrastructure and facilitate a growth in tourism, which becomes the most important economic sector in the country.
The drachma, the oldest currency in the world, is replaced by the euro in 2002. The new, "hard" currency gives Greece easier access to financial resources, which many politicians are unable to resist. Unnoticed, huge mountains of debt are accumulated, which are used to service widespread clientelism. In the financial crisis after 2008 these debts can only be squared by extensive financial bailout measures on the part of the European Union. The economic reforms which the money lenders demand in return lead to social unrest and a new party landscape. In 2015 hundreds of thousands flee to Europe from the Middle East via the Greek islands. Greece faces major challenges.

Santoríni

The very dry and, in summer, hot volcanic island is quite unlike the other Cyclades. Situated in the South Aegean Volcanic Arc, the island has been repeatedly undergoing massive eruptions for 200,000 years. The last big earthquake was in 1956. Increased volcanic activity has been measured again since 2011. Its present-day appearance dates back to the eruption of a volcano beneath the originally atoll-like limestone island about 1650 BC. This was the greatest catastrophe in the history of mankind. An up to 60 metres thick layer of pumice tuff ejected by the eruption was deposited on what remained of the island. In this layer are now found the typical valleys formed by erosion with cave dwellings.
The top destination of world tourism is not necessarily a "must" for hikers too. Since most of the island has developed a good network of roads and tracks, it is rather difficult to find secluded trails. Santoríni is characterised by its sunken mule tracks bordered by black lava stones and grey sand, as fine as icing sugar. Shady trees are rare; the landscape is dominated by vineyards. The bus connections are reliable and serve the start and end of all the walks described. The taxi prices are mostly excessive and can hardly be bargained down.
Walking tours 1, 5 and 6 are particularly recommended.

Thirassía, the island lying opposite, has remained rustic – even without any places for visitors to stay. Yet the tight time frames of the boat connections from Oía do not permit proper hiking excursions. Besides, in the northern part of the island the lanes are mostly concreted and the mule tracks largely overgrown.
Hiking maps: Anavasi #10.24 Terrain # 313
Nakas Road #108 (1:35.000)
Taxis: +30-22860-22555/23951

❶ Cliffhanger

The classic Santoríni walk: 4 hours on the edge of the precipice with spectacular vistas and a super picnic area! The well constructed footpaths are marked "1", "5" and "9".

■ ***9 km, difference in altitude 130m, easy – moderate***

AWT The tour starts at **Fíra** archaeological **museum** and leads
0.00 past the famous viewing points, first through the **Fíroste-**
0.05 **fani** district. Up to here the tavernas stand cheek by jowl.
Beyond the fortified nunnery Agios Nikolaou (viewing
0.20 possible) you proceed to **Imerovígli** with the baroque bell
tower and castle ruins on the rocky promontory. Having taken some steps upwards to the right, you turn left at the war memorial and left for 10m at the end of the square. Then right to an elongated car park and on between hotels. At the end of the town [1] you take the trail at the
0.35 edge of the crater. After a dip, with **cemetery** and hotels,
0.50 the path gradually ascends and **forks** at the hotel com-
plex *Pantheon Villas* (**P1:** N36°26.963'/E25°25.467', 360m).
0.55 Rising up on the right is the later main trail.

★ *On the left you can drop down to the* ***Antonius Chapel*** [2] *in five minutes, a resting area the like of which one seldom comes across in the Cyclades. It has everything: picnic tables, a cool grotto with frescos and even a little WC building.*

Lying peacefully in the middle of the crater is the island Vulcano, which only emerged from the almost 400m deep caldera 300 years ago.

The general backdrop was created by the greatest natural

disaster in human history. The huge volcanic eruption took place around 1650 BC, destroying in one go the island's Therean culture. That is when the strait between Thirassía and Oía, situated on the right side, emerged.

Unwillingly dragging yourself away from this belvedere, you climb back up to the main trail, where you keep ascending beside a church (left). Almost on the peak stands the church **Profitis Elias.** You saunter down the edge of
1.05 the precipice along a paved-gravel path in good condition to the **road**, which you take for a quick 250m.

1.10 Beside the kantina, renowned for freshly pressed oranges, an elegant mule track leads up the Negolo Vounó (Black Mountain). Awaiting you on the second summit is a **chapel** with a fine view of the northern part of Santoríni.

1.40 Now you descend dramatically on lava in the direction of Oía, past a second chapel [4], which bears the name of the Prophet Elias.

Alternative: If you wish to **bathe**, go right, down the footpath below the Elias chapel, across the road and into pretty Finikía, then follow ② to the sea and to Oía.

At the edge of Oía, on the left after a hotel, is a humming **water desalination plant**, which above all supplies the
1.55 precious liquid for the numerous swimming pools. A path along the side of the slope leads on past a few of these to Perivolas Market at the road. Going left here and left up the steps in front of the **St. George's Church**, you traverse
2.10 the churchyard to arrive at the main road from **Oía.** On it you later follow the stream of tourists which is drawn – like us – to "Sunset point".

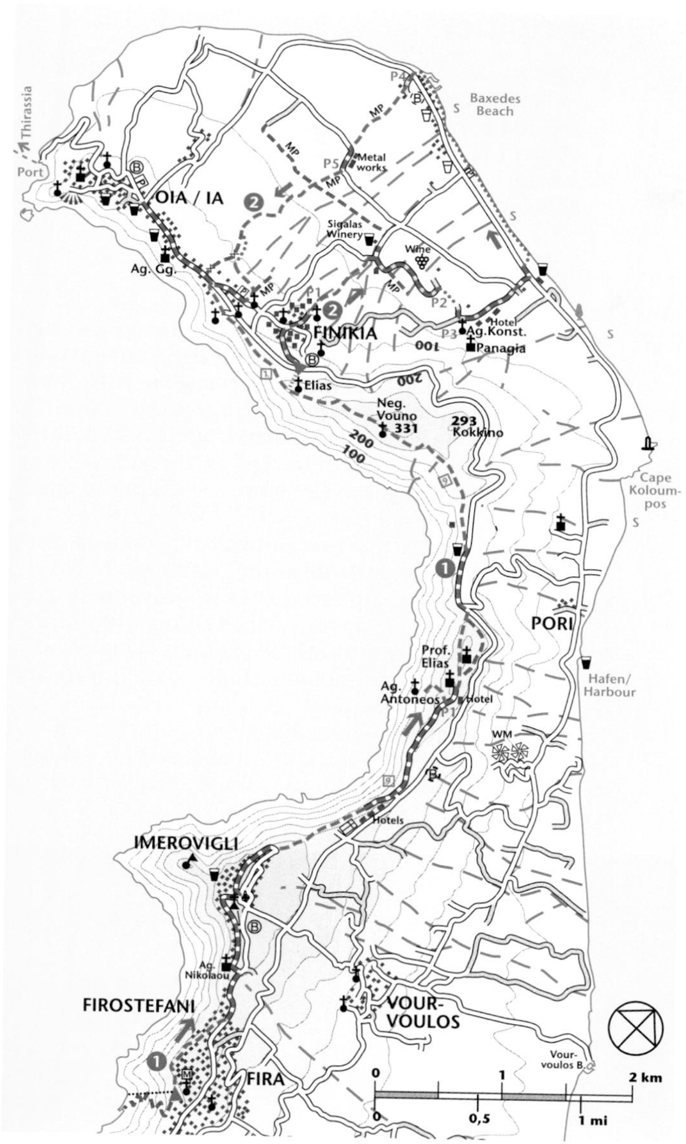

Thirassia
Port
OIA / IA
Ag. Gg.
Baxedes Beach
Metal works
Sigalas Winery
Wine
FINIKIA
Hotel
Ag.Konst.
Panagia
Elias
Neg. Vouno
331
293
Kokkino
Cape Koloumpos
PORI
Prof. Elias
Ag. Antoneos
Hotel
Hafen/ Harbour
WM
Hotels
IMEROVIGLI
Ag. Nikolaou
FIROSTEFANI
VOUR-VOULOS
Vourvoulos B.
FIRA
0
1
2 km
0,5
1 mi

❷ Sandpipers

This 3½-hour hike leads from the pretty little village of Finikiá down to Baxédes beach, continuing back to Oia up a somewhat overgrown monopatí. Along the way it is possible to taste wine, bathe and – in season – also drop in for a bite.
■ 3 km, difference in altitude 160m, easy

▷ *Map see previous page*

AWT From the bus stop on the main road a village alley takes us
0.00 down into quiet, picturesque **Finikiá.** Over to the right
stands a church. At a fork we descend right, then contin-
ue right on the same level [1] and further downhill. The al-
0.05 ley forks in front of a **wooden door.** Here we follow the
0.09 signs to the music café **"Potamos"** (**P1:** N36°27.913'/
E25°23.623'). It is the last building in the village. Wine
cellars have been dug into the pumice cliffs of the gradu-
ally widening valley.
The renewed footpath [2] leads down to the coastal plain,
which is dominated by viniculture. Having reached the
0.20 small **side-road,** we are faced with a question of con-
science: Is it still too early for a wine-tasting sortie?
For just 100m further towards the sea is the wine-growing
estate *Sigalas,* where one could taste the new vintage and
order a few titbits in the pretty garden.
Those with misgivings immediately turn off right on to a
lane which, after a house (right), makes several right-an-
gle bends. At the third one is a small stockyard on the
right (**P2:** N36°28.270'/E25°24.010').

Further down the lane ends and one proceeds right, up the well-beaten track towards the Panagía Church on the slope. Later a lane runs in the same direction to the small
0.35 **Constantine Chapel** at the foot of the mountain (**P3:** N36°28.290′/E25°24.236′).

From here we stroll seawards, past the Pelagos Hotel (right) to a side-road and on to the coast road. Going left along this for 80m as far as a shallow dip, we arrive at
0.45 **Baxédes beach** without any difficulty.

Heading west, the beach walk on the black-and-white sand initially leads alongside impressive pumice cliffs into which boat-sheds have been hewn ③. Unlike real sandpipers we do not look out for washed-up flotsam and jetsam, but a nice place to swim. Then we saunter on to the
1.10 **harbour** and up to the coast road.

15m to the left, opposite a wayside altar near a culvert, a roadway runs inland (**P4:** N 36°28.876′/E 25°23.202′). At the following left turn-off we notice a mule track running straight ahead ④. It is open to traffic for a short distance beyond a locksmith's (left), before turning off right at a
1.25 left-hand bend between **two electricity poles** (**P5:** N36° 28.407′/E25°23.279′). Having passed a crossing of the paths, our path is sunk into the terrain – and more and more overgrown.

300m before our destination, the houses in Oia, we have to surrender and stomp onwards without a path on terraced meadows. Where the overgrown path forks (down right), we encounter a path leading up left. At the top it brings us, outside "Maria's Place", to a side-street which we stroll along to the right. On the main street we go
1.55 right again to the **St. George's Church** of **Oía/Ia.**

③ Erosion

The eroded valleys, almost as typical of Santoríni as the caldera precipice, are little known. From the small St. Mary's church on the "kasteli" you have a view over the largest of these valleys. In the north, towards Fíra, lies Vóthonas behind such a valley. Our route is quickly planned: we will climb down from the kasteli through this eroded valley to Vóthonas, from there past the airport and on to bathe in Kamarí. It should not take more than 3½ hours.

■ *7 km, difference in altitude 365m, easy to moderate*

AWT The Perissa bus takes you to **Pírgos**, the capital of the island until 1800. Take a stroll through the old, winding lanes up to the kastéli, the Venetian fortress from 1663. Here your gaze can roam far over Santoríni.

Below the kástro, with the noteworthy St. Nicholas
0.00 church behind you, start at the **obelisk** and 15m beyond it, down 12 steps. Walking past the noble Hotel *Zannos* (right), you come to a church 1 and just before it go right, down the paved path. Later under a flying buttress and right at the fork down to a concrete ramp to the left
0.05 which joins a **road.** Going right along it for 40m, you take another concrete ramp down to the left. Later the ramp will become a concreted winegrowers' path, sunk in to the ground and a pleasure to walk along.

The sizeable road which follows hardly bothers us as, ten metres further on to the right, our path continues on down into the eroded valley (**P1:** N36°23.226'/E25°

1

2

27.039', 270m). A little overgrown in places, but passable. The typical black Santoríni surface accompanies us until we have left the vineyards and enter the pumice gorge. Prickly pears stand on the wayside of the deepening eroded valley. For centuries the winter rains have been filing away at the pumice deposits, which are up to 60m thick. At a cave- chapel ② we reach **Vóthonas** and take the concrete track leading down right, with typical cave dwellings still in ruins after the earthquake of 1956, when some 3000 houses were destroyed on the island. The caves are ideal for their inhabitants – cool in the summer and warm in the winter. On the left at the entrance to the
0.25 village stands the large **Panagía church** with a huge eucalyptus tree.

Alternative: If, before the Panagía church, you go up into the valley on the left, only eight minutes away is the locked cave church **Panagiatis Sergeinas** which acted as a hideout during pirate raids in the Middle Ages.

From the eucalyptus tree on the right beside the Panagía church you proceed left up into the small town and right in front of the next church. Later comes a classicistic house on the left ③. Below the windmill you go right and down the stairs to the valley and there head left. The domed church with the nine enormous bell-cotes dominates the village from up here. Passing some more partly
0.30 renovated holiday cave dwellings, you go to the **end of the village** before leaving the eroded valley via numerous bends. On the right a twin cave church of St. Prokopius has been dug out of the slope; shortly after you reach the
0.40 **main road** next to a taverna.

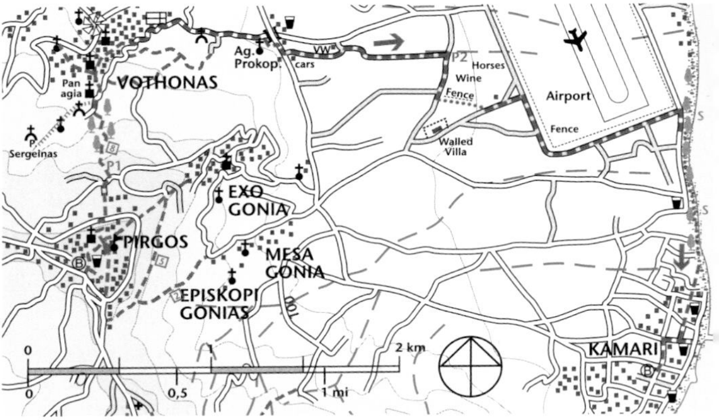

In front of the bridge you work your way up right and take the main road to the right for one minute. Opposite a tyre workshop and in front of a used car dealer we again devote ourselves to hiking. Having passed a Volkswagen dealer on a dirt track, we are quickly back in the nature. The dirt track leads towards the sea, until it comes to
0.55 **transverse track** (**P2:** N36°23.588'/E25°28.320'). Straight ahead a dry-bed runs down to the sea. Here we take the dirt track *to the right,* towards a large futuristic building [4]. Who on earth could dwell behind those enormous walls? We will never know and, 150m before the wall, turn off left at the end of the vineyard (left), without a path. Keeping to the right side of the vineyard, you reach a dirt
1.05 track, which leads left to the **airport perimeter fence.** Strolling alongside this, glad that you are not sitting in one of the planes taking off, you cheerfully arrive at the
1.20 black **beach** of **Kamári.**
Shuffling right for 10 minutes pretty much alone, you
1.30 come to the **first inn,** soon to be followed by many more on the road running alongside the sea. At the last one, the Mango, though, you should cease your search and turn off to the right. In the next road on the left you will find
1.45 the **bus stop.**

④ Ancient Théra – Never on a Monday!

Along with Akrotíri and Délos, the ancient site of Théra, founded in the 8th century BC, is the main archaeological sight on the Cylcades. This trek leads in 4 to 5 hours across the saddle of Mt. Messavounó with the excavations – which are however closed on Mondays. You should set off with enough time left to fit in with the opening hours (see below).
■ 8 km, difference in altitude 350m, moderate

AWT It is a half-hour bus journey to **Empório:** sit on the right-hand side of the bus, as the views are often breathtaking!

*The houses of the **kástro,** the old town higher up, are joined together like a castle on the outside and linked by a maze of narrow lanes within. You enter through two covered passages.*

To find where our trek will continue later on, you should first take your bearings on a terrace below the kástro (at the exit marked "1831"). In the fields on the outskirts of the town, at the foot of the mountain to the south-east, is a church with three vaults. Approximately 80m to the right of it is our subsequent route.

From the terrace we descend the steps past the large church (right) and down into the dip. On the road you go twice to the right, down 200m before turning left be-
0.00 tween two barrel-roofed **storehouses** [1] on to a narrow track leading up a slight incline. 100m ahead on the left is the stump of a windmill. On the left above the terraces is the three-vaulted church of Agios Taxiárchis which we could already see from above.

0.05 Having turned on to the **dirt track** which comes down from the left, you leave it again at the second bend to the right, after a electricity pole 2 (**P1:** N36°21.443'/E25° 27.095') bearing left on to a path which runs horizontally to a retaining wall. Going along it, you come to a house with the Iríni chapel with three bells (left). After a few steps you come across a narrow road, which you should take for 60m to the left. On the right before a quarry you will see a rural lane, along which you head on to a **group**
0.12 **of houses** (right) and a bend in the road (**P2:** N36°21.467'/ E25°27.485', 50m), where you go left and then straight on.
0.20 Skirting past a **dwelling with chapel** (left), you go left for 80m along a lane and, later at the fork, left along the foot of the mountain. A few workshops are located here. Périssa stretches along the coast to the right; the island of Anáfi is visible in the distant background. Ahead of you is the rock on which Ancient Théra lies. If you take a closer look, you will discover a small Panagía chapel, built daringly into the rock.

After a right-hand bend you come to a road where, past the waiting riding mules, you go left. At the foot of the
0.30 mountain is the **upward path** 3, metal sign: now the ascent can begin.

The track up to Selláda, as the saddle is known, is fairly steep but can be managed in half an hour. (A partly exposed path leads off right to the Panagía chapel in the
1.00 rockface.) A kantina awaits us in the **saddle** above. Except Mondays.

*If you want to visit **Ancient Théra**, you should be there by latest 2.30 pm, as visitors have to leave the site by 3.00 pm. The site has well-preserved remains of buildings dating* *from the Egyptian-Ptolemaic era (250 BC) and subsequent Roman times. The excavations were carried out around 1900 by German archaeologists, who also left the descriptions. The position of the town facing the sea is particularly impressive.*

Anyone itching to go for a swim can take a minibus from here to the coast. But, never on a Monday.

The route for pleasure-seekers, who should however be fairly steady on their feet, leads to a path heading away from the road to the left at the third right-hand bend.

↙ The superb hiking trail runs along the mountain high above Kamarí. Later on you come to the cave-chapel of
1.15 **Zoodóchos Pigí** ("life-giving source") 4 via some steps.

★ *A picture-book site such as can only be found on the Cyclades: in the grotto a masonry table for the visitors to the parish fair and bells hanging in the branches. A heavenly peace reigns up here, only a short way from the hustle and bustle in Kamarí. Even though the life-giving source cannot serve its function, because the cave is barred.*

The road is paved from here, leading down over hairpin
1.30 bends to the black beach of **Kamarí.**

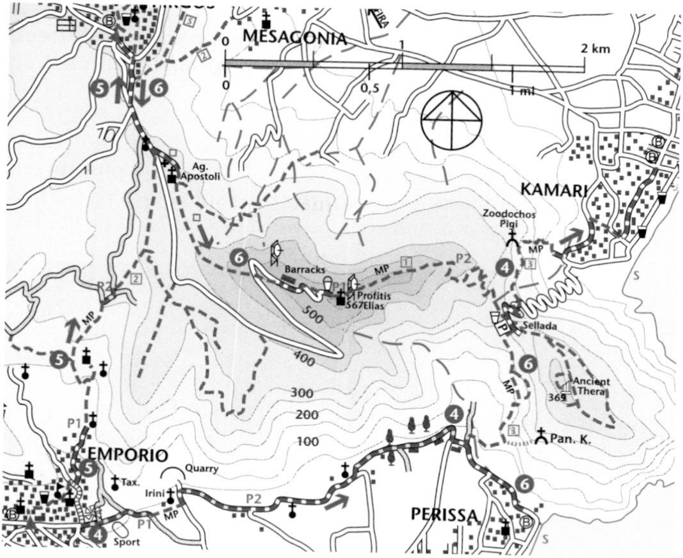

⑤ Ascent to Pírgos

This 1½-hour walk can be done almost exclusively on old mule tracks – a rarity on Santoríni. They are marked "2". Gentle climbing and two interesting small towns, each with a kástro, make it a charming outing. The only taverns are to be found in Empório and Pírgos.
■ 4 km, difference in altitude 285m, easy – moderate.

Combined with walk 6 makes this into a three to four-hour, yet difficult tour.

▷ *Map see previous page*

AWT Take the Périssa bus as far as **Empório** and alight at the square below the large church. First walk on the same level, then, in front of the classicist school, left up the paved path as far as a transverse path. Go right there, keep "straight ahead" and, after a church with dark basalt walls (right), left up to the gate of the kástro from 1831 (p. 29).
0.00 Having explored the place, you descend from this **gate** between the kástro and the domed church until you come
0.05 across the church square to an alley. Go right to a **street.** At the distributor on the left at the corner you turn left up to a valley.
0.12 At the end of the village a **chapel** (**P1:** N36°28.406'/E25° 23.279') gives us its blessing before we leave the parish just beyond two flying buttresses. A delightful old sunken
0.15 pathway leads us on down in to a valley. Where it **forks** 150m below a monastery [1], we start climbing to the left

in zigzags and on up along a ridge [1].
0.30 Do not be disheartened by the wide **dirt track** to the right, which has to be followed uphill for 100m, for 20m beyond a right-hand turn-off you can proceed up beautiful steps and an old mule track on the right (**P2:** N36°22.140'/E25°26.961', 270m). To the left lies Megalochóri and later ahead of us the hill village Pírgos. Gradu-
0.45 ally ascending the slope, we finally reach the **road** near the first houses in Pírgos.

Prolongation: If you go downhill from here for about 30m, you will come to a wayside cross and the path up to **Profítis Elías monastery**. Description ⑥.

Otherwise one stays on the road and, after a dip, you
0.50 leave to the right to **Pírgos** bus station.

A wander through the narrow streets of this hill village, which was the island's capital during Turkish times, is an absolute must. The Venetians left one kástro here.

⑥ The aerial monastery

The monastery of the prophet Elias has dominated the highest point on Santoríni from time immemorial. The military aerials which have been added in modern times may have disfigured it, but they have also made it unmistakable.
The great charm of this 3-hour hike lies in the distant views and the almost entirely intact old mule tracks. On top of this come the excavations of Old Théra as a cultural bonus. You will miss tavernas along the way, though. Sporty hikers can start in Empório and follow tour 5 first.
■ ***7 km, difference in altitude 560m moderate – difficult***

▷ *Map see page 31*

AWT Setting off from **Pírgos** bus station, walk along the even
0.00 alley from the Café Johnny as far as a car park. Where this
ends, go left 5m and then down the paved alley to the
0.05 **road.** About 150m up this you will see a **wayside cross** on
0.10 the left of the road, which has now started to climb. Here
a sign marks the old footpath up to the monastery which
later passes the Apostle church [1]. Following the moun-
0.30 tain ridge, walk straight uphill until you reach the **road**
again. Directly opposite a short path commences, only to
terminate at the road again further up. On the road, be-
low the barracks, you should proceed as far as steps (left)
which lead uphill past the water tank from 1941 (right).
0.40 The road brings you to the **monastery**, which – surround-

1

2

ed by transmission masts and radar equipment – offers a most curious motif for a photograph.

*The **Profítis Elías monastery** was built between 1711 and 1857. The interlocking complex has no courtyard of any significance. Coming in out of the dazzling light, it takes a while to make out the beautiful fittings in the dark monastery church. The contemplative breather in the cool interior of the church is a godsend. Sadly the monastery is mostly closed.*

0.40 Leaving the **monastery grounds** through a large metal
door, we follow the road for a few metres up to the right.
Below the abandoned military building you leave it
through an opening in the wall to the left (**P1:** N36°22.115'/
E25°27.796', 565m) Those with a pronounced fear of
heights may find the first two hundred metres rather try-
ing ②. It gets easier after that. Even dwarf pine grows in
this windy region and offers at least optical hold. Later a
1.00 wide pumice track leads to a **stone pyramid** (**P2:** N36°
22.237'/E25°28.248', 435m) Further down artistically
1.20 arranged double bends lead us to the car park in **Old Théra.**
It lies in the saddle, Greek "selláda", in front of the moun-
tain Messa Voúno. During the summer a kiosk does busi-
ness here.

It takes ten minutes to reach the top of the excavated Ptolemaic city, but entrance is only permitted up until 2.30 pm – except on Mondays. Read more about the excavations on page 30.

Alternative: if you follow ④ from AWT 1.00, you come to **Kamári**, which has very good bus connections with Fíra.

Beside the kantina begins a gravel footpath to Périssa, which soon passes the recently discovered cemetery of Old Théra. To the right on the mountain stands the whitewashed monastery.

Daring hikers can take a fifteen-minute detour to a chapel in the precipitous rock face by taking a steep path on the left/straight ahead.

Having arrived down on the coastal plain, you should fol-
1.40 low the road to the left in order to reach **Périssa** and the
sea, where buses leave for Fíra.

It is also possible to wander along the foot of the mountain for half an hour as far as Empório and then catch the same bus from there.

⑦ Vineyards

In the south of Santoríni are expansive vineyards which we want to roam through. Partly using surfaced tracks and dirt tracks we visit the elegant village of Paleochório and later the coast near Akrotíri in 2½ hours. The excavation sites are open until 8.00 pm in summer. Rest points are available.
■ 6 km, difference in altitude 260m, easy

AWT To reach the starting point, take any bus going to Períssa, Akrotíri or the "Port". Be sure to make it clear to the driver that you want to get off at the crossing in front of the "Suites of the Gods" (or also "Antonou winery"). This crossing lies 600m *beyond* the "Santos winery".
0.00 At the **crossing** is a chapel on the right. Directly opposite you saunter down the concrete track, avoiding the glowering 'Rottweller' by taking a sunken path on the right, which runs delightfully downhill ①. On the following
0.05 **concrete track** continue in to peaceful **Megalochóri.** Below a large church (left) an alley leads through a bell arch
0.10 to the pretty **platía** with several inns.
From there we continue beneath the bell tower down the street, disregarding turn-offs to the right. Below the vil-
0.15 lage we rejoin the familiar **path** (**P1:** N36°22.403'/ E25°25.930'; 70m). Although this has unfortunately acquired a concrete cover for quite a long section, it soon passes through the vineyards, bordered on both sides by walls. Lying directly on the pumice ground, the roundly bent vines are in a better position to draw the night wetness from the loess soil. This is where the famous "crater

wine" originates.

After passing a cistern
0.25 (left), cross under the **road** to Périssa and continue along the dry concrete stream-bed, all the time heading towards the sea. Walking alongside a construction storage site and past a cistern (right), you
0.45 reach the chapel **Agía Anna** [2].

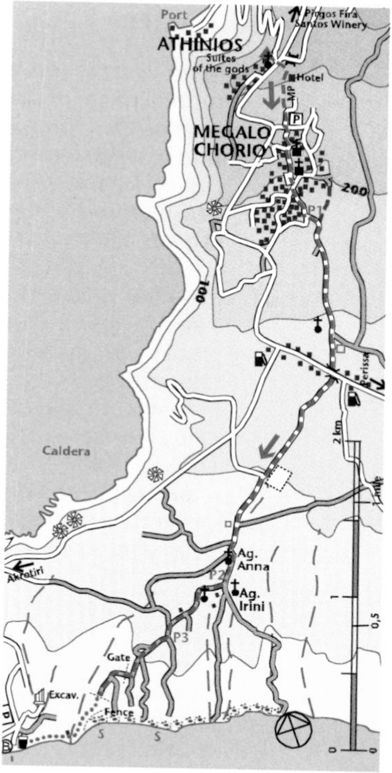

In front of this a lane takes you up left and, three minutes later at the fork near the Irini chapel in the vineyard (left), to the right (**P2:** N36°22.406′/E25° 25.919′) in the direction of the village of Akrotíri. Surrounded by fields and vineyards with tiny winegrowers' houses, you amble straight ahead at the fork in front of a house (right) and round a left-hand bend.

Then a right-hand turn-off at a gate in a fence takes you downhill (**P3:** N36°21.169′/ E25°24.815′). At a turning place for cars (right) go straight ahead, then right (so not into the ravine) and through a fence gate. At the next fork the same procedure: Go right and not to the sea.

This leads you to a fence and, on the left, you are relieved
1.05 to discover a **gate** and path. Disregarding the next fence to the left, well-beaten tracks on the left side of stream-
1.10 bed bring you to the **sea.** On the left is a lonely, but stony beach.

Keeping to the coast, you come to the bus stop and on up
1.15 to the **excavations of Akrotíri** (see next page) For those who are not in a hurry there are also plenty of nice inns down by the water ...

⑧ Akrotíri

After visiting the Minoan excavations, you climb up to the village of Akrotíri, wandering first along the edge of the crater, before reaching the flat seaward side of the island mostly on dirt tracks. You can choose between two beaches and a tavern. Total duration about 3½ hours.

■ ***8 km, difference in altitude 230m, easy to moderate***

AWT Take the bus to the **Akrotíri excavations.**

The ***Minoan excavations of Akrotíri*** *are one of the greatest archaeological sensations of the last century. The uncovered parts are 3500 years old and the two layers underneath are said to be as much as 8000 years old. A free plan is available at the ticket office. Open in peak summer until 8.00 pm.*

0.00 The trek begins **above the car park.** To the left of the entrance starts a sunken path marked "12". After two minutes it passes under a bridge. With a view of Akrotíri [1] you work your way along the foot of the slope. Going
0.15 right, you walk across a valley bottom up to the **road,** turn right there and, behind the car park (right), up left to the bus stop in Akrotíri. Bearing left uphill from the bus stop to the neo-classical school, you continue in the direction of the beak of the eagle seated on the monument. After 30m steps lead in to the Venetian kástro with panorama café – and bagpipe museum.

From these steps you go straight past the church (right)
0.20 and head up to the **road.** You remain on it for 100m until you reach the hairpin bend, where a lane with steps leads

you on uphill to the left. Take the first lane on the left, going past a lowered chapel square (left) and a tight cluster
0.25 of houses. At the end of the village is another **chapel** on the left.

Here you go right along the concrete road up to a fork (minimarket on right), and then left. Continuing on through the next group of houses, you turn right on to a narrow concrete track which is lined by stone walls on
0,30 both sides and come past an outstanding red **villa** [2]. 100m before and below it begins a path (**P1:** N36°21.532'/ E25°23.493', 160m). At the next bend we have the mag-
★ nificent panorama of the "inland sea" with the three towns Oía, Thíra and mountainside Pírgos.

The mule track leads us further, almost without any effort on our part, later above the road, to a twin chapel. There
0.40 is a sign leading down a stepped path to **Panagía Kinísi** (**P2:** N36°21.697'/E25°23.196', 145m). Ahead of the paled gate of this pilgrimage church we bear left on to the mule track towards the lighthouse on Cape Akrotíri. Below the mountain peak to the south-west is a chapel [3] – in a while our resting spot!

You wander on over the flat, between the vines growing on the ground. Perhaps we should try some of the island wine this evening! It thrives here because the volcanic

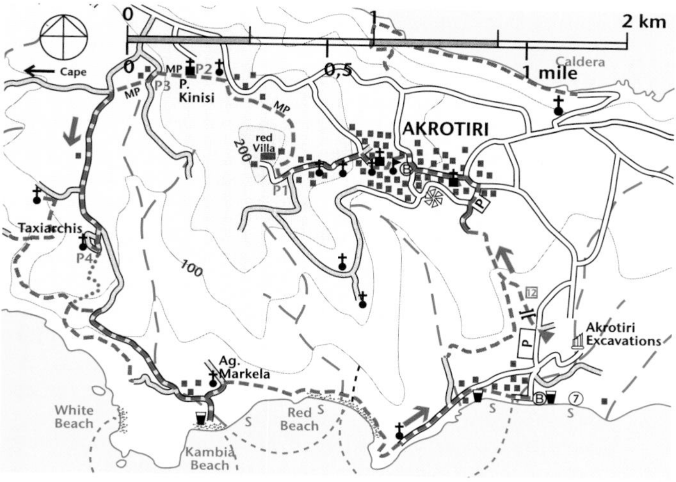

3

4

rock is particularly fertile and the pumice absorbs the dew, then releases it gradually. The grape harvest takes place as early as the end of August.

In front of some houses a dirt track crosses ahead and you follow it left for 80m. At the left bend (**P3:** N36°21.651'/ E25°23.057', 145m), bear right on to a hewn path. Then
0.45 go left on the next **dirt track.**

Our main route leads towards the chapel on the rock. The dirt road offers little for the eye – just ordinary countryside. Yet soon we come out of our visual depression: we
0.55 take a few minutes to walk up to the locked **taxiarchis** (archangel) **chapel** (**P4:** N 36°21.290'/E25°23.909', 105m) and do something here for our spiritual welfare and against our thirst. Besides blessing every drop of water from the cistern, Saint Paraskeví also restores poor eyesight. Those with eyes in their heads will spot several unsightly blights on the open landscape.

To avoid the dusty main track below, you can leave the roadway leading down there before in a bend to the left. A rather indistinct path on the right skirting the mountain and descending into a dip. Then it is only a short distance
1.05 down along the dusty **track** to the seldom frequented
1.15 "**Kambia Beach**" with grey sand and shady tavern.

Anyone looking for a more lively beach should walk 100m inland, right at the fork and to the right of the wall. On the level of the Markela capel (left) turn right to take
1.35 the path to "**Red Beach**" 4. Despite the numerous sunshades and sunbeds, it offers little in the way of catering. In the summer kaikis are available.

Over the red cliffs and then along the sea with good tavernas you arrive back at the **bus stop** near the water.

Sífnos, Panagía tosou nerou

Sífnos

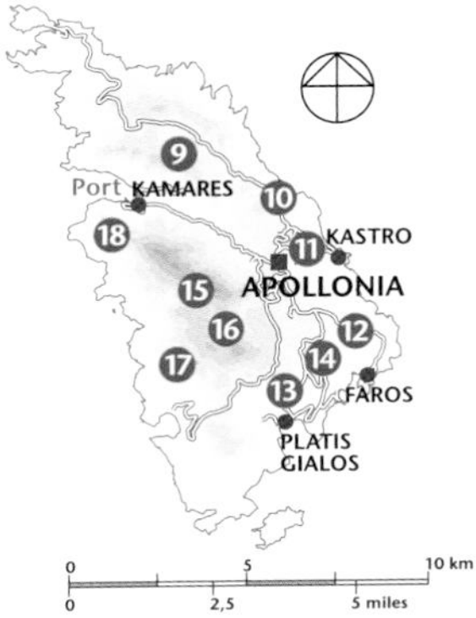

Two mountain ranges of white marble run through the fertile green island. Beds of silver-containing ores made it one of the richest islands of the Cyclades in Antiquity. Mining was carried out up until one hundred years ago. The lower-lying areas mainly consist of mica schist, a sandy sedimentary rock raised from the sea. The coastline is mostly rocky with interspersed bays in which one encounters sandy beaches.

The lush vegetation with numerous olive groves and the many gently sloping mule tracks still in use make Sífnos one of the most popular islands for Cycladic walkers.

Apollonía, the high-lying picturesque capital town, is the best place from which to set off on walks; thanks to their good bus connections, though, Kamáres and Platís Gialós can also be recommended. However the island's easy accessibility from Athens can lead to accommodation becoming overcrowded at weekends.

The noticeably large number of well-kept trails through the delightful landscape pass countless open monasteries, 235 chapels and some wells. In addition the villages, each with its own character, provide worthwhile destinations for the walker. Above all the southern part of Sífnos is visited and explored on foot by stalwart regulars. And good bus connections guarantee a safe return from every trek.

The island administration has cleared and marked eight hiking trails, which are marked on the Anavasi map. Of the hikes described here numbers 10, 15, 18 and 19 are to be especially recommended.

Hiking maps: Anavasi # 10.26, Terrain # 304
Nakas Road # 10, Sifnos Trails (Municipality of Sifnos)
Taxis: +30- 22840-31925 6932-403 485
Private rooms, hire cars: Thesaurus, www.thesaurus.gr

❾ High above Kamáres

Those who can spare 3½ or 5½ hours will experience one of the most beautiful walks on the Cyclades. Using wall-lined mule tracks, we explore the picture-book landscape around Apollonía. A good well (P2) awaits us at the half-way point. From there it is possible to shorten the hike and concentrate on enjoying the more striking sections. In the lower part a couple of places are sometimes overgrown – which is why long trousers are an advantage.
■ 8/12 km, difference in altitude 145/430m, moderate/difficult

AWT A stair-path, the skála, leads up to Artemónas from beside
0.00 the old-fashioned "Café Lakis" on **memorial square** in
Apollonía (175m). Up on the right is the large domed
church of Petáli, from where the path leads to a hollow
0.10 and right to a **bridge.** The steps lead uphill again to the
elongated square in **Artemónas.** To the left of the shady
taverna "Margerita" the lane continues straight on for
about 150m through fashionable Artemónas with its attractive gardens and manor-houses.

You go left at a house blocking the way. On the right after
0.15 100m is a well furnished **church** directly on the lane and,
50m further on the left-hand side, the large church of
Kóchi with its blue dome. 20m behind this you have to go
down the gentle incline on your left and the alley on the
right at the fork. The antennae are up on the right as you
leave the houses behind you. Some 350m after the church
0.20 of Kóchi you reach the **end of the village.**

Later we notice metal signposts, which we follow: ΑΓ. ΣΥΜΕΩΝ/Agios Symeon! With each step the deeply cut path becomes a dream monopáti, we're strolling rather than hiking [1]. After a well (left) it becomes rocky underfoot for a while until we reach a dirt track, where we
0.30 must not forget to take the right-angled **left turn** (**P1:** N36°59.204'/E24°42.846', 280m). The metal sign is 10m after the fork.
Head for the two summit churches on the horizon, then go down and turn left at a fork. On the right in the middle
★ of the fields is the Dimitri Chapel [2] with a cistern. After a
0.35 **hollow** the mule track meanders idyllically along the slope, we bear towards the summit chapel of Ágios Lázaros and finally drop down slightly to the large fountain Trispiges (right) hewn into the rock to the right of the path (**P2:** N 36°59.696'/ E 24°42.467'). From there you
0.55 walk to the **bottom of the valley.**

> ***The short cut to the Lázaros chapel*** drops *left 20m on the valley floor* and then right, up a beautiful monopáti to the small settlement below the chapel. The path to the chapel (235m) is sometimes overgrown.
> From it one can either walk back again or, from AWT 2.30, take the tour described below.

To reach the St. Simon monastery, go 100m up a roadway
0.55 on the right in the **valley floor** and, in front of a modern cistern, to the left and up a splendid stair-path [2].
Unfortunately, the attractive steps turn into a scree path further up, but we have come a good bit closer to our destination, Mt. Simon. To the left of the path you will see
1.10 the former iron ore mine of **Voríni,** which is now filled in with rubbish.

> *This was one of the five ancient mines on Sífnos. The iron ore found here contains a lot of silver. In the 5th century BC slaves lying prostrate in their shackles drove the narrow tunnels into the mountainside, advancing 30 cm a day. The silver then made Sífnos the wealthiest Aegean island. Iron ore working was re-commenced in 1900 and continued into the 1920s (see below).*

1.10 Above the landfill we use the roadway as far as the road, which we stride up to the right. After 300m, next to a
1.15 **small house** (left) (**P3:** N36°59.981'/E24°41.868', 325m), we find the path "7", which leads between wall and road
1.25 up to a **water reservoir** (right) (**P4:** N37°00.042'/E24°

41.469′, 350m). *To the left of this* we re-encounter the old pilgrim's path through juniper bushes, which we follow (going left at where the concrete track curves) as far as the
1.45 **summit monastery Ágios Símeon** (480 m).

It lies far removed, high above the sea. As soon as you enter
★ *the courtyard, the view pans out across the open, glittering sea. A place of absolute tranquility.*

The first stretch back from the monastery is the same as the way up. Shortly after crossing the concrete track for
1.55 the second time at the **hairpin bend**, you should turn off

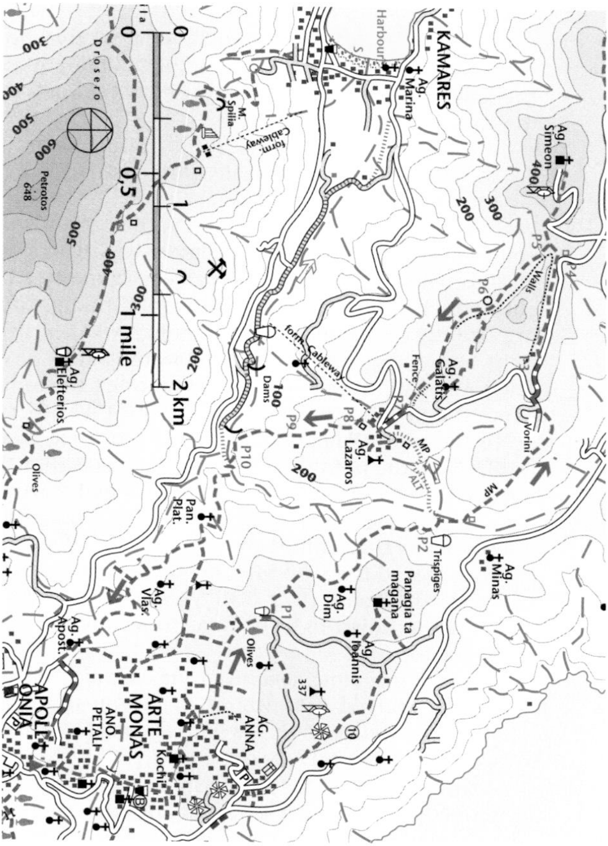

to the right (**P5:** N37°00.031′/E24°41.415′) away from the well maintained part of the paved path, about 60m before the reservoir. The path continues below the walls running towards us on the slope ③.

> ***Alternative:*** Those who suffer from *severe* vertigo should also use the already familiar track for the return leg.

Proceed along the clearly visible path marked with pale colour dots, past the pen (left), later keeping at a distance of 40m below the dry walls. First you come to a broader path which then becomes a horizontal hiking trail leading through elder bushes. The Kamáres valley is on the right, sometimes steeply right below the path.

The route flattens out whenever you reach the remains of a round lime kiln (**P6:** N 36°59.833′/ E 24°41.662′) and go up to the wall. (You should *not go through the gap* in the wall!). Now the path slowly descends between bushes, always in close proximity to the wall on the left. Apollonía has come into view on the horizon, in the foreground the houses below the summit church Ágios Lázaros.

Having opened the steel mat directly beside the wall, you
2.30 come to the **road** (**P7:** N36°59.596′/E24°42.044′) and march 200m down right to **two stone towers**, which taper at the top.

> *The towers are the remains of the summit station of the former material cableway of the Voríni iron ore mine. Along the route of the present-day road ran a railway which served to haul the ore.*
>
> ***Alternatives:*** Should you wish to avoid the trail described below which is, especially in spring, covered in vegetation, you could follow the road as far as

Kamáres or take the alternative route back to Apollonía described from AWT 0.50 in the opposite direction.

Immediately to the left of the stone towers you descend to a wide iron gate, beside which you clamber over the low fence. Tramping downhill alongside the wall on the
2.35 left, you turn left after 80m (15m below a **house ruin**) (**P8:** N36°59.477'/E24°42.083'). The first stretch of the trail is sometimes a little overgrown in places! Without
2.50 turning off, you come to a small iron **gate** (right) (**P9:** N36°59.310'/ E24°42.150). Above this on the left stands a house. Beyond it the path might be heavily vegetated again. Continuing downhill, you arrive, after a left-hand
3.05 bend, at steps winding their way down into the **stream-bed** (**P10:** N36°59.054'/E24°42.271').

Walking upstream to the left, we see the stone pyramids neatly piled up on the rocks and the no less artistic flight of steps hewn into the rock mass. Now comes a five-
3.10 minute steep ascent, but this is mitigated by a first **view of Katavatí** from up above.

Five minutes beyond the Panagía chapel on the right we
3.15 come to a **fork**, where we proceed straight on. (Going left would bring you up to Petáli.) Later the path starts to
3.25 climb a little. At a **fork**, above which on the left stands a St. Blaise chapel, we likewise turn left. Following a short
3.35 ascent we are greeted at the top by the **domed chapel of the Apostles** (right) [4].

Very soon we are surrounded by houses, after which we go left up the road and then, before reaching the hump, right on to a footpath at the braced power pole. Alongside a chapel (right) we reach the *skála,* and further down the
3.50 main square in **Apollonía.**

To Kamares:

3.05 From **P10** (AWT 3.05) you go right in the **stream-bed** into the main valley and then out of the valley. 50m below the first weir a roadway commences on the right. It goes round the left side of the second weir. On the coastal plain a roadway runs first to the right, then to the left of
3.45 the stream-bed to **Kamáres.**

⑩ Above the sea

This 3-hour panoramic tour, marked "1" and "8", starts from Kástro, first along the coast, then on raised ground above the sea. It mostly leads along old paths and hence away from any tavernas. By walking through a green valley, you come to Apollonía via Artemónas.
■ 8 km, difference in altitude 250m, moderate

AWT From the isthmus outside **Kástro** you wander below the
0.00 **windmills,** at first on a road along the coast , then uphill
at the fork. (On the right beside the sea the sewage plant.)
After 100m, to the right of a perimeter fence, you find a
glorious path on the left which meanders between two
★ narrow walls half way up the terraces above the sea [1].
Contentedly, you arrive first at a chapel and then at the
0.20 former monastery **Panagía Pouláti.** Below the church, di-
rectly on the path, you may like to enjoy a Cycladic
resting spot in a small, walled garden ... gentle terraces
which you never tire of seeing lie between here and Ká-
stro. In severe heat it is worth taking three minutes to nip
down to the spring by the rocky shore.
Directly ahead of the car park begins an ascending
kalderími. The picturesque old stair-path (B2) is thrice se-
vered by the dirt track. You can use the Agios Loúkas
windmill above as a bearing. Go left round the house at
0.30 the second interruption of the path. Cross the **road** at the
small holiday houses. The path takes you past the resto-
red windmill (right) of Agios Loúkas and ends in front of a
stockyard up on the level ground. Bearing right here, you

soon see a wonderfully situated cemetery on the right.
Continue straight ahead on the road in a northerly direc-
tion and left at a junction.
Below the village of Artemónas (with windmill) you turn
!! *right* after a left-hand bend in the road (on the right are
0.40 two elongated holiday houses) on to a **wall-lined track.**
This forks after 100m in front of a semi-detached house.
To the left of this you discover a gently ascending stair-
path. It later runs below a tall retaining wall, then 200m
horizontally to steps and the road (**P1:** N36°59.162'/
E24°43.566'). Go down this 40m and then take the old
0.50 flagstone path up left to **Agía Anna.**

Short cut: By going left along the valley in Agía Anna, you can reach Apollonía in 25 minutes via Artemónas.

In the village our route takes us first right, up into an al-
ley. The hill with the aerial masts, at the foot of which is
0.55 another **cemetery**, rises up to the left. 100m later you
turn off the dirt track to the right. This is where the won-
derful, peaceful panoramic way "8" heads to Sóstis, high
above the sea, following the contour lines. Antíparos and
Páros lie on the horizon. The demarcation formed by the
wall on the left-hand side of the path is missing for a whi-
le. Where the wall reappears further on, a steel water pipe
has been laid. Finally the path veers left, heading inland,
1.05 towards a **dirt track.**
Turning your back to the sea and going left in a southerly
direction, you find yourself on a plateau with the Panagía
ta Magána monastery to the right on the opposite slope.
Once again, who other than Prophet Elias keeps watch
over it all! On our way between the field walls we come
1.10 past a **St. John's chapel** [3], then continue straight ahead,

1.15 past a **left turn-off.** The walls are getting higher here and,
1.20 at a **fork** (metal sign to Symeon Monastery in the opposite direction), we go left.

Between the high walls [4] appears Artemónas. But before reaching it, you come to major forks along the way: at the first you go down to the left, at the second up to the left and right at the one in front of a metal gate. Now you only have to resist the temptation posed by the shady taver-
1.35 nas on the oblong square in **Artemónas**, in order to get
1.50 safely back down to **Apollonía** via the steps of the splendid skála.

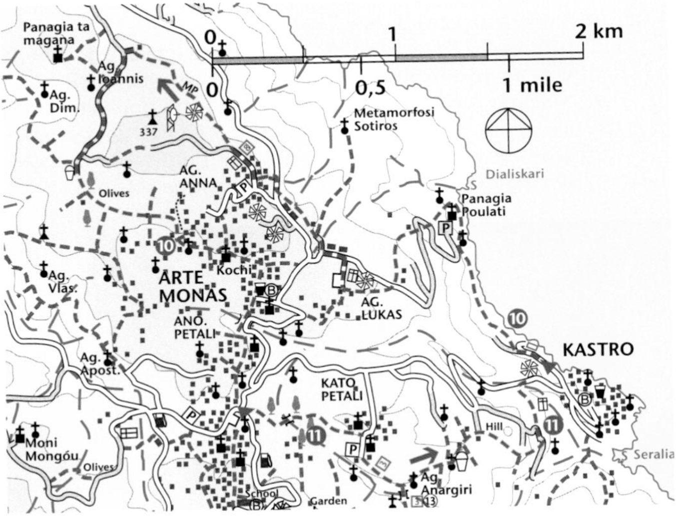

⓫ From Apollonía to Kástro

This tour of 1½ hours leads through varied, agricultural landscape on the eastern side of the island, heading along solitary Cycladic trails to Kástro, the medieval capital, where it is possible to join walk 10.

■ ***3 km, difference in altitude 180m, easy***

▷ *Map see left*

AWT To the left of the raised site with the war memorial on the
0.00 **platía** in **Apollonía** a lane next to the snack bar leads into the maze of houses. We follow it for 40m to a stair-path which leads down to the left, pass beneath the road and then 70m later go down to the right. Soon coming into view on the hill opposite is the wonderful paved track "3" to the village of **Káto Petáli** 1. After a valley dotted with
0.05 olive trees you cross a **bridge** into the village, but it re-
0.10 mains up on your left. At the far end is a **large church** with a blue dome. Descending a few steps to the right, you go across the car park and head straight along a narrow concrete path on the other side to a sort of suburb. Here you proceed down a slight incline and then – opposite a chapel on the other side of the valley 2 – left above the valley. Having passed a dovecote tower (right), you bear left (red dot) at a T-junction up on to a beautiful Cycladic trail. (Track "3" leads to the right here.)
0.15 Soon you see the **twin chapel Anargýri** 3 between the trees on the right, where you turn off left again. After 120m come two forks within 10m of each other: bear left

at the first and right at the second! The xirolithíes walls on either side are quite enormous. 50m beyond a flat-roofed chapel (right) you turn off first left and then right
0.20 between **two houses.**
After passing the driveway to the house on the right you continue straight ahead along a monopáti towards a hill. Before the hilltop the path veers to the right, loses height and crosses another mule track. That is where you turn off left, walking downhill with a splendid view of Kástro [4]. Down below runs a dirt track, which you follow for 50m to the left, when you find another monopáti on the right. Passing above the cemetery, this brings you down to the eroded rocks in the valley and up to the road and the
0.45 windmills. On the left a lane leads up to **Kástro.**
If you prefer to take a dip first, walk on until you reach Serália, Kástro's harbour, with a tiny beach and a taverna.

Since Antiquity the capital of the island was Kástro, which received its present appearance during the Spanish-Venetian period. The abutting houses are built so as to form a fortress with 5 passages which curves around the lens-shaped centre with its narrow lanes and churches by way of protection. The finds from the ancient acropolis are on display in the small archaeological museum.

12 From Fáros to Kástro

This 2-hour tour, marked "2", can be used to prolong walk 14. It is also recommended in its own right.
■ 4.5 km, difference in altitude 140m, easy

AWT In **Fáros** you ascend the step-path in the higher western
0.00 part between the two beaches, passing the Nicholas chapel at the end of the village. The wide paved path, which used to form the main connection to Apollonía, leads up
0.10 through treeless fields on terraces and becomes **flatter.** Go
0.15 up the **dirt track** which then comes for about 30m, until you rediscover the already familiar monopáti on the left, which later takes you past the solar installation (right) to
0.25 the **road** (**P1:** N36°57.173′/E24°45.030′).
Proceed up the road to the left for 120m, turning off on to a monopáti on the right 20m opposite a water reservoir. After eight minutes the monopáti divides on an expansive area with a cattle-trough (left) (**P2:** N36°57.519′/E24° 44.733). Climb up to the left there, taking the horizontal path to the right after 50m. Further on you find another cattle-trough (**P3:** N36°57.316′/E24°44.868′), where you
0.40 go right across the **valley bottom,** then left up the hill to the small Nikitas chapel [1]. Silence reigns, apart from a humming sound from an electric generator up above.
Stroll on between high walls leading through olive gro-
0.50 ves, turn up to the left at the next **fork** (**P4:**
★ N36°58.008′/E24°44.508′, 340m) and after that straight
0.55 ahead until you **catch sight** of Kástro [2] at the end of the defile. In the valley are steps straight ahead of you leading
1.15 up to **Kástro** (see p. 52).

1

2

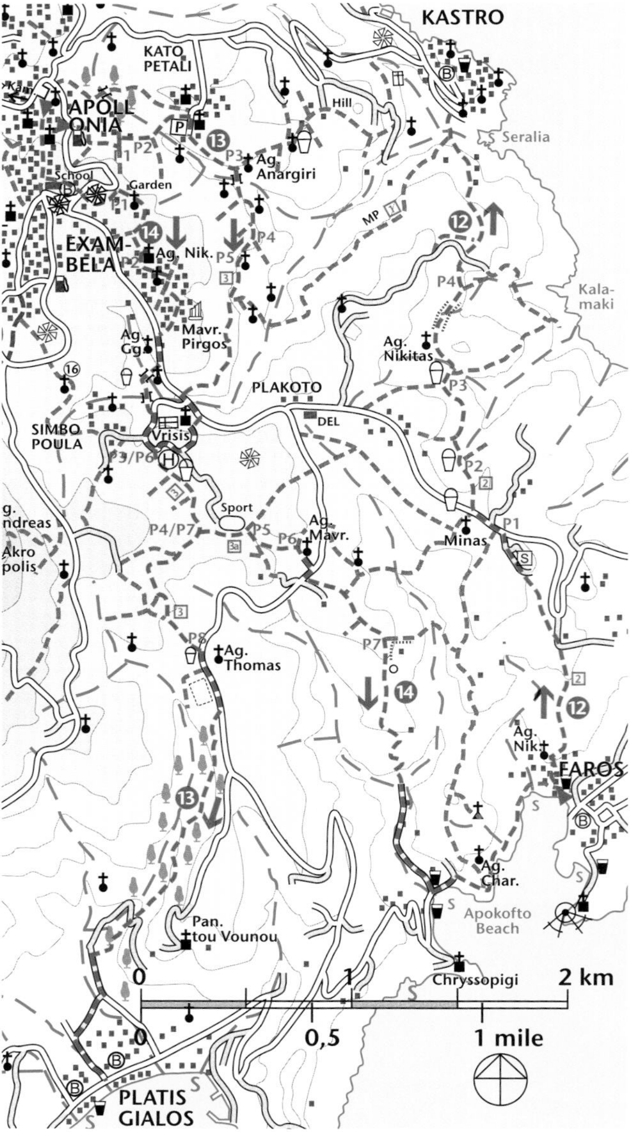
KASTRO
KATO PETALI
APOLLONIA
Kam.
Hill
Seralia
Ag. Anargiri
School
Garden
MP
EXAMBELA
Ag. Nik.
Kalamaki
Mavr. Pirgos
Ag. Gg.
Ag. Nikitas
PLAKOTO
DEL
SIMBO POULA
Vrisis
P3/P6
Sport
Ag. Mavr.
Minas
P4/P7
P5
P6
P1
P2
P3
P4
P7
P8
Ag. Thomas
Akro polis
Ag. Nik.
FAROS
Ag. Char.
Apokofto Beach
Pan. tou Vounou
Chryssopigi
0
1
2 km
0,5
1 mile
PLATIS GIALOS

⑬ Moní Vrísis

This 3-hour tour leads through terraced agricultural land from Apollonía to Platís Gialós. Apart from one short section of road the walk only follows old mule tracks, which is what makes it such an experience. Along the way we pass the large fortified monastery of Vrísis, the only one that is still inhabited and open until 12.00. Its romantic inner courtyard is an ideal place to relax. From there we drop down to the sandy beach of Platís Gialós.
■ 7 km, difference in altitude 180m, moderate

▷ *Map see left*

AWT Immediately to the left of a **petrol station** on the eastern
0.00 edge of **Apollonía**, on the road to Fáros, you go down a narrow lane. After 15m turn on to the concrete path on the right and, after another 100m, bear left up old steps. At a house on the left at a bend, proceed until you come to a transverse lane at a shed (left). Here you first turn downhill to the left and then, 30m further between two
0.05 houses, horizontally to the **right** (**P1:** N36°58.317'/E24° 43.659', 195m). The annoying concrete surface soon ends, the route reverting to a proper path between high dry-stone walls; later it goes down 1 in the direction of Káto Petáli. Go left at a T-fork (**P2:** N36°58.285'/E24°
0.10 43.864'), traverse the **dry bed**, turn right below the village and right again at the car park next to the large church as far as a little valley.

At the edge of the valley, whose right-hand side is marked

1

2

by a beautiful chapel, you pass a dovecote (right). At the
0.15 **T-junction** (**P3:** N36°58.204′/E24°43.945′, 150m) follow the "3" down to the right across a little bridge. The path starts climbing again and runs on the right above the stream. At the fork go left up the steps to a cube-shaped
0.20 **chapel** (left). Spread out on the left is a classic Greek terrace landscape, criss-crossed by old country paths.

Go left at the following fork and right at the next one (**P4:** N36°58.101′/E24°44.080′, 160m). (Kástro can only be half glimpsed from this vantage point). Dream on through the cornfields with olive trees until you come to a flat-roofed
0.25 **chapel** (left) [2] (**P5:** N36°57.999′/E24°44.070′). From the forecourt you can see cars driving past further up.

If you follow the path, you reach a fork with signposts. (Down to the left is the direct route "1" to Kástro.) Continue straight on until, after a bend, you behold the massive fortified monastery of Vrísis ahead of you [3], while Agios Andréas greets you from above. Soon you reach the road, where you go left for a bit and then up the well-
0.40 worn steps to **Panagía Vrísis monastery.**

The son who came from a very short relationship between a nun and a sailor founded this fortified monastery, which is only inhabited by two monks now, in 1654. If you proceed beneath the cell block you come out in to the picturesque inner courtyard dominated in the middle by a cruciform domed basilica with valuable fittings.

From the monastery gate a roadway leads uphill and on
0.45 up to the right, to the **helicopter landing place** (**P6** (+P3): N36°57.495′/E24°43.787′, 225m). To the right of this the wall-lined track "3" runs towards the sea, dividing on the level of the football field (left) (**P7** (+P4): N36°

57.301′/ E24°43.928′). Proceed to the right along a wonderful mule track [3] and then left down to the road (**P8:** N36°56.998′/ E24°43.935′, 190m).

From the well there you walk along asphalt for 400m to the right. (Do not take the first path on the right *in front of* the fence.) After this fence a path leads to the right, initially without accompanying wall, into a green gorge. Accompanied by water pipes but with very little else of any interest, the trail runs along the left side of the slope.

Down on the coastal plain the path is again lined by
1.35 **walls.** At ten concrete steps you turn off the by now wide
path into a narrower one on the right. Soon you reach the
1.45 700m long, yet extremely narrow **sandy beach of Platís**
Gialós. In low season you will only encounter few visitors.

⑭ The landmark

A downhill walk of 3½ hours from Apollonía to the church of Chryssopigí, the island's landmark, also boasting attractive tavernas and a bathing beach! Possible to extend with ⑫.
■ 6.5 km, difference in altitude 230m, moderate

▷ *Map see page 54*

AWT To the right of the snack bar on the **main square** of **Apol-**
0.00 **lonía** you walk 40m to the main alley "Odos Prodou" (s. p. 19), which leads up right.

30m ahead of the large domed church, on the right, is the
0.05 *noteworthy flat-roofed church of* ***Agios Sóstis*** *(1768) with a picturesque forecourt.*

Level with the last steps is a high wall of the grammar school on the left. *Before* it you turn left on to the narrow path – first walking downhill, then to the right up to the
0.10 **road.** On the other side continue left after two windmills and right before the bend of the road. In front of a well-kept garden (**P1:** N36°58.164'/E24°43.696') commences a rising monopáti.

Skirting the left-hand, seaside edge of Exámbela, you pass
0.15 a shady **chapel** ① and after a swing to the left come to the
0.20 **blue domed church** of St. Nicholas (**P2:** N 36°57.997' E 24°43.752', 230m), immediately beside which you enter an alley on the left. Your way leads down right at the T-fork in front of a row of houses and then left again 5 m further on. This track, which soon starts to drop, first heads towards the sea, then right and later past the re-

1

2

mains of a circular tower in a farm on the left. The
"Mavros Pirgos" (black tower), was built in the 3rd to 6th
century BC without mortar using precisely hewn stones
and served as a refuge and for transmitting light signals.
0.25 Further downhill you come to the **road**, which you fol-
low, past a St. George's chapel (right), down to the left for
about 220m before leaving it again to the right (200m fur-
ther on stands the large Vrísis monastery from 1654).
0.30 **Steps** lead down from the road past a chapel (left) to a
monopáti and two bridges in the valley. At a washing
place you come to a concrete track. We follow this up
right. Above on the left is the cemetery chapel. When the
concrete track forks, you head left up to the **helicopter**
0.35 **landing pad** (**P3** (+P6): N36°57.495'/E24°43.787').
40m beyond the pad you make your way right into the
realm of the monopátia and towards the sea. A ruined
windmill keeps watch on a hill to the left and the vast St.
Andrew's monastery resides above to the right. High walls
on the right-hand side of the path guide you reliably
ahead. You stroll on over pleasant paving stones, past a
0.40 **cistern** (left).
At a fork (**P4** (+P7): N36°57.303'/E24°43.931', 230m) take
the path "3A" down left and later, alongside the football
0.50 field, to the major **fork** (**P5:** N36°57.467'/E24°44.132').
Going right here, you enjoy the fine sea vistas. At the next
fork you follow the wide track dropping left towards the
sea. A domed chapel comes into view. At the T-fork above
the road (**P6:** N36°57.291'/E24°44.271', 200m) go right as
1.00 far as the **Mavroundi Chapel** on the road. Far below the
church of Chryssopigí on the rocky peninsula is already
discernible.
After crossing the road on a slant to the right, you wander
up the trail to the *left of a dirt track*. Disregard right-angled
turn-offs on either side. Go straight ahead at the *edge of a
wall*, then *down to the right* before a wall with gate at a fork
(**P7:** N 36°57.024'/ E 24°44.514'). The going becomes
rather steep down to a dry stream-bed, from where a
sandy path leads you out to the shore.
1.30 ***Chryssopigí church*** *[2], which dates from 1650, possesses
a miraculous icon. On the rocky promontory, directly above
the sea, stands a baptismal font. A "place of strength".*
1.45 Stroll on along the coastal path to **Fáros**, which also has
beach and tavernas – and the bus.

⑮ Summit coffee with St. Elias

The steep 400m ascent to the highest monastery on Sífnos is rewarded by a stunning view. The 3½-hour trek can be combined with tour 16.
■ *9.5 km, difference in altitude 515m, moderate*

▷ *Map see page 64*

AWT If you do not wish to use the main alleyway in Apollonia,
0.00 as described in tour 17, you can also opt for this alternative:
From the **Platía Heróon in Apollonía** (175m) you go down the road to Kamáres for two minutes and, immediately after the water ditch (opposite the car park), up a few steps to the left. From here the alley in the Kourtsoúdi dis-
0.05 trict leads straight on uphill. You only go right at a **junction.** Shortly after that a new chapel can be seen on the left behind a wall, while you continue uphill in the direction of a large domed church. 50m before this church you go left and come to a slight hollow.
0.10 At the edge of **Katavatí** village, which soon appears, you keep left, coming to a transverse road, where you turn up right. Soon after you walk below the domed church (p. 65 [1]) and follow the village street. Rising up to the right is our destination, the mighty mountain of the Profítis Elías. Next to the route on the left is the Hotel "Galini", a little later on the right a chapel with an elegant memorial slab in the forecourt.
100m further a sign points the way to the right, leading to
0.25 the information stand on the **by-pass road.**

Cross this on a slant to the right, where you hit upon an-
other mule track leading uphill (**P1:** N36°57.803'/
E24°43.231'), which takes you into the interior of the is-
land above a valley (right). The following turn-off (**P2**) to
0.35 the left is described as tour 16. Our **turn-off to the right**
to the Profítis Elías lies in the bottom of the valley across a
concrete ford (**P3:** N 36°57.562'/E 25°42.804', 270m).
It is not difficult to find the path through mastic and ju-
0.50 niper bushes. Next to the path on the right is a **refuge**
(390m), from where you can see the Elias monastery
1.05 again [1]. After passing a **shed** (right), you notice it gets
flatter before becoming steeper again on the ascent up to
1.20 the **monks' fortress** (682m).
OW

The monastery of the ***Profítis Elías o Psilós*** *("the tall one"), which now stands empty, was probably founded in the turmoil of the iconoclasm around the year 800. The present-day buildings were erected around 1650. It is assumed that there was already a watch-tower here during antiquity. This highest point already served to defend the island in those times.*

The centre of the rectangular complex is marked by the kathólikon, the detached church. It possesses an interesting iconostasis made of stone, into which the illustrations are inserted.

On the outside of the building, below the monastic cells, are casemates with embrasures. In the main building are the refectory with a long stone table, a cistern and further embrasures [2].

And a friendly invitation to brew up coffee...

To return, use the same way or join ⑯.

⓰ The Mycenean Acropolis

Besides the Elias monastery it is the summit church of Saint Andrew which dominates the centre of Sífnos. In pre-ancient times a huge acropolis stood here. Following paths and mule tracks on the 3 to 4-hour hike, we explore the green central part of the island and also visit the excavation sites. These are one of the island's main attractions. No watering-places exist on the entire route.
■ *8 km, difference in altitude 240m, moderate*

AWT Follow walk 15 or 17 as far as the **by-pass road.**
0.20 From the nature reserve's information stand it is 30m to the right across the road to the path leading to Profitis Elias (**P1**). After about eight minutes on the paved track you leave it at wooden signs pointing left to Anargíri chapel (**P2:** N36°57.698'/E24°42.966', 300m).
The mule track [1] ascends gently through juniper bushes, passing through a metal gate after a quarter of an hour
0.45 (**P3:** N36°57.397'/E24°43.009', 370m) and reaches **Anargíri Chapel** [2]. This is consecrated to the saints of medicine Cosmas and Damian, who took no silver (argíri) for their treatments. Above it can be seen the destination of the tour: the circular wall of the acropolis.
!! Immediately after the chapel *the trail forks indistinctly:* we climb up left and come on the narrow path to the car park
0.50 and, further up, the **museum.** Although small, it provides a lot of information, finds and aerial photos. From there a new footpath leads beneath the circular wall up to the excavation sites.

The double, rampart-reinforced wall encircling the acropolis was built in the late-geometrical period (8th century BC). 500 years earlier a Mycenean settlement had already existed here for 100 years. So far the ground-plans of about ten houses have been exposed 3. *The ongoing excavations will surely reveal further details. The monastery was constructed in the 16th century, mainly using stones taken from the ancient walls, much to the displeasure of the archaeologists.*

0.50 From the church of the former monastery (nice picnic
1.05 spot) you take the steps leading down to the **road**, where you go to the right for about 120m and then to the left along a sand track. 70m on you turn on to a mule track, also on the left (**P4:** N36°57.170'/E24°43.878'). This sweeps elegantly 4 past a chapel (right) and down to the
1.15 hamlet **Simbópoula.**

Before reaching the first houses you walk left along the dirt track which later, concreted over, runs downhill to a right-hand bend. In the middle of this bend (**P5:** N36°57.559'/E24°43.603', 245m) you turn off to the left on to a wonderful old footpath which first snakes round a small valley, then rises and leads past a chapel (left) up to
1.30 the **road** (**P6:** N36°57.750'/E24°43.436').

The path continues on the other side until it comes to the
1.35 **edge of Katavatí.**

You are now on familiar ground again: below the village church you go right and, at Apollonía grammar school,
1.50 down to **heroes' square**, Platía Heróon.

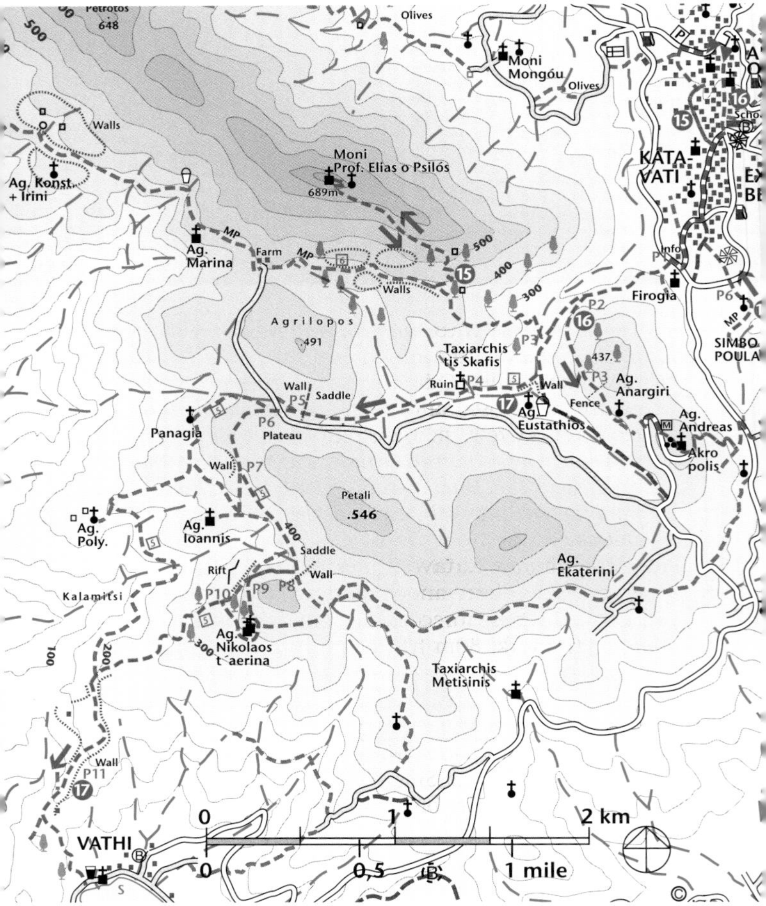
Petrotos
648
500
Olives
Moni
Mongóu
Olives
Walls
Ag. Konst.
+ Irini
Moni
Prof. Elias o Psilós
689m
KATA-
VATI
Ag.
Marina
MP
Farm
MP
500
15
400
Walls
300
Info
Firogia
P2
16
P6
MP
SIMBO
POULA
Agrilopos
491
437
Taxiarchis
tis Skafis
P3
Ruin
P4
Wall
P3
Ag.
Anargiri
Fence
Wall
Saddle
P5
17
Ag.
Eustathios
Ag.
Andreas
Akro
polis
Panagia
P6
Plateau
Wall
P7
Petali
.546
400
Ag.
Poly.
Ag.
Ioannis
Saddle
Wall
Ag.
Ekaterini
Rift
P10
P9
P8
Kalamitsi
Ag.
Nikolaos
t aerina
300
200
100
Taxiarchis
Metisinis
Wall
P11
17
VATHI
0
1
2 km
0
0,5
1 mile

(17) At the Foot of the Prophet

This 4-hour route, marked "5", is easy to follow and leads through the nature reserve at the foot of Profitis Elias. For relaxing at the end of the trek, taverna chairs on the sand and the beach of the quiet bay of Vathí await us.

■ 9 km, difference in altitude 420m, moderate

▶ *Map see left*

AWT The day begins at the **main square in Apollonía**, at the
0.00 narrow passage next to the snack bar which leads into a
narrow alleyway. After 40m you bear right, up the pic-
turesque main alley Odos Prokou (see p. 19). The bou-
tiques are still closed and the chairs of the tavernas up-
turned. Yet a few people are already having their
breakfast. During the week all the churches are closed, in-
0.05 cluding the large **Metropolis Church** (left). At the upper
end of the stair-path head right for a few metres along the
asphalt road, leaving it again at the signpost to Katavatí.
0.10 You go left below **Katavatí church** [1], then on past the
0.15 hotel "Galini" (left) and the church of **Panagía An-
gelokísti**, in whose forecourt lies the moving epitaph of a
pope. At the fork, 80m further on, signposts point right
towards Mt. Elias. You head straight on downhill over
concrete, then through an olive grove on to the informa-
0.20 tion stand at the **bypass**, which you follow right for 30m
before climbing up some steps (sign "Elias") (**P1:** N36°
57.803'/E24°43.231', 235m). Not much can go wrong from
here on, and there are blue marker dots into the bargain!

1

2

The wall-lined track you now use lies on the slope opposite Mt. Elias [2]. First comes a turn-off to the left to
0.35 Anargýri chapel (**P2**) ⑯, then, in the hollow, the **trail** to Profítis Elías turns off to the right. (**P3:** N36°57,562'/E25°42,804', 280m) ⑮.

Our route "5" continues straight upwards here. Later, in front of a wall below a chapel [3], it turns right up into a
0.45 high valley, where the Archangel and his church, **Taxiarchis tis Skafis** [4] (**P4:** N36°57,417'/E24°42,574', 420m), soon appear amidst some ruins. If it is open, you can see some beautiful, though badly damaged frescoes in the chancel, or bema. Some of the monastery terraces in the valley are planted with vines, watched over from above by the fortified monastery of the Prophet Elias. Above the eastern/left-hand end of the valley you can make out the acropolis site at the St. Andrew's monastery, though the monastery itself cannot be seen.

Attractive steps lead on to the high plateau. 20m beyond the gate in the saddle (**P5:** N36°57.340'/E24°41.966',
1.05 390m) you go left at the **fork.** After 120m you cross a dirt road and go left at the fork which follows (**P6:** N36°57,354'/E24°41,823', 420m). Here trail "5" divides into an upper and a lower part.

!! We use the ascending path *to the left.* At first it has a concrete paving and later, after a wall, becomes a red-coloured scree track. 30m after a rounded wall the track
1.15 **forks** (**P7:** N36°57.240'/E24°41.725'). We take the path
!! going *left,* which runs parallel further up and follow the contour lines, our eyes fixed on the white, domed church (B5) which lies on the right, below the next peak. Down to the right lies the St. John's monastery. A huge crevice is

5

6

visible on the opposite slope. Which one of the Greek Gods raged here?
1.25 The path forks 40m before a **long wall** up in the saddle (**P8:** N36°56.876'/E24°41.949'). We go right and follow,
1.30 on the same level, the curves of the next hill. At the **fork** to *the left* of a wall (**P9:** N36°56.852'/E24°41.794') we take a detour to the left, winding our way through the juniper
1.35 bushes to the monastery **Agios Nikoláos t'aerina** [5]. The large courtyard affords a magnificent view across Vathí bay.

The beaten track down to there descends through tall bushes below the monastery. After 4 minutes (**P10:** N36°56.786'/E24°41.684') you again encounter trail "5", which you go down to the left in bends and through a gate. On gravel you walk in bends through juniper bush-
1.50 es. After the **two trails** "5" have rejoined each other, you head towards a wall. Here you swing right and descend through lateral walls. The right one later drops down to a farmhouse in the valley. You set your sights on Mílos, the island furthest to the left. After the walls again become
2.05 **narrower** (**P11:** N36°56.943'/E24°41.266') there are attractive spots for a picnic in the olive groves. 40m beyond the fence gate at a house (left) you turn off left [4] and
2.25 soon reach **Vathí.** Several beach tavernas await your arrival!

The narrow sandy beach is right next door. To reach the bus, you have to walk 100m inland. The last bus leaves at 4.20 pm in spring, and as late as midnight in high season. If you still have time: At the end of the bay the pottery Atsonios has tasteful wares on display.

⑱ The watery monastery

Far away from everything, at the island's outer extremity, stands a little abandoned monastery. This 7 to 8-hour walk marked "6" can be started in Kamáres or Apollonía. On narrow tracks it skirts Mount Elias, passes over the mountain ridge and descends to the sea. The continuation to Apollonía leads high above the sea along the foot of the mountain. En route are three further monasteries. Water can be drawn from cisterns at two places and one well.

■ ***12/14 km, difference in altitude 300m, difficult***

AWT **a) Start in Kamáres:**
0.00 Inland, to the right of the main street, is the **Hotel Ka-**
0.07 **mari**. From there a concrete road runs up to a **reservoir.**
This is where the trail marked "6" begins, leading round
0.20 wide bends up to **stone steps.**
Then the path becomes more slippery. Walk on past the turn-off (**P1:** 36°59.054'/E24°42.269') to the *Mávro Spiliá* cave. Although the path comes to juniper bushes further up, it has been cleared well. After two minutes it passes
0.35 the remains of a round **ancient signal tower**, ten meters to the left (**P2:** N36°58.982'/E24°40.983', 330m). Ten metres in diameter, it is now only one metre high and has two access stones ①. Sífnos boasts the remains of 55 such towers. In case of danger they served to transmit alarm signals.
Later, on the left, you see two of the pylons of the materials cableway from the ore mine, then a large house ruin

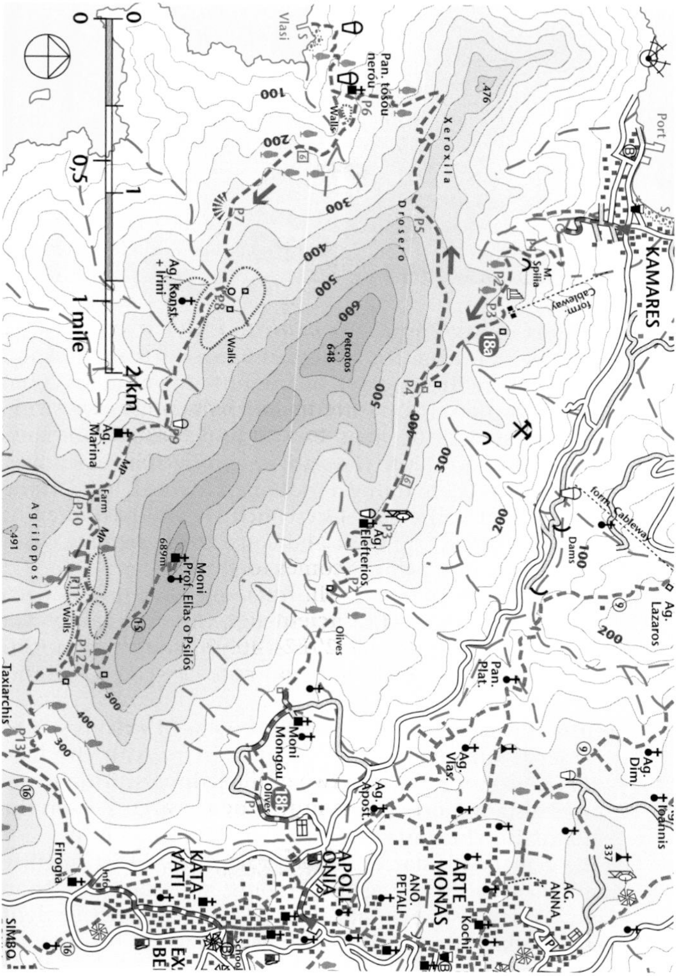

(**P3:** N36°58.640′/E24°41.259′). The easily discernible path first runs horizontally along the hillside, then up to
0.55 the **water reservoir,** below the main track (**P4:** 36°59.049′/E24°40.695′) Here is the AWT 1.10 of the route described below.

b) Start in Apollonía

0.00 Here we start from the tree-lined **heroes' square** in **Apollonía**, where the road to Kamáres runs downhill for 200m
0.02 past steps (left). Opposite the **car park** (right) we swing left and ascend the steps leading up to Matzourini lane. But we turn off this to the right after only 30m, at a power pole, and proceed along a monopáti marked "6". On the hill in front is the cemetery which we will pass later. At
0.05 the next fork we go right and come to an **asphalt road**, which we cross diagonally to the right.

After that our route heads down along some houses (left) and through the bed of the stream, then to the right of the "homely" dovecotes [2] and uphill along a monopáti
0.10 to the **cemetery.** Dead easy, the walk can go on like this for ever!

From the cemetery we command a view of what is still to come [3]: our first goal is the monastery with the blue dome on the left in the foreground, the next one is the more distant monastery with the radar reflector up on the mountain. The route looks more difficult than it is!

The gravel path starts off level, veering left, then slightly uphill. After 200m, again climbing, we take the second mule track (**P1:** N36°58.031'/E24°44.735') on the right and, walking up through olive groves, rejoin the now familiar gravel path. We walk along it to the right and then down to a crossing, where, after passing through the por-
0.25 tal, we turn right down to the former **monastery Theológos ton Mongóu.**

The 400-year-old monastery used to accommodate society ladies who failed to live up to the good reputation of their families. It is now in private ownership. If the owners hap-

pen to be present, visitors are still most welcome to have a look round the church with its very beautiful "baroque" iconostasis.

Back at the crossing above the portal we go straight on up the dirt track. 20m before a water reservoir (left) we are relieved to discover a wall-lined path on the right heading towards our goal on the mountain. Further on some
0.40 clumsily repaired concrete steps lead up to **ruined houses**
!! (left). 80m after these we turn *sharp left* beside high walls (**P2:** N36°58.517'/E24°42.120', 285m).

0.55 More steps lead up to the **monastery Agios Eleftérios.** Inside the plain church the visitors' book reveals when the last hikers passed through here. We have a choice between water from the cistern or ouzo from the table. It still exists, filoxenía, Greek hospitality. Unfortunately, though, it is too early for a swig from the bottle – after all we are bound for the watery monastery!

In front of the radar reflectors walk to the left (**P3:** N36° 58.604'/E 24°41.936'), along the slope [4]. Below the path can be seen the upturned brown masses from the ore mining and a cavernous pit. Standing guard on the mountain range opposite, above the Kamáres valley, are the summit monasteries of the prophet Elias (left) and Saint Simon.

1.10 In the meantime we have reached a **reservoir** (**P4:** N36° 58.734'/E24°41.323') on the right-hand side below the path, serving as a point of reference. The path from Kamáres comes up here (see above).

1.25 Later we cross the mountain crest of **Xeroxíla** (**P5:** N36° 58.719/E24°40/713', 420m), which means "dry wood". Before we dry out ourselves, we had better leave the windy saddle. A superb view of the island opens up: in the background the lofty Mílos, in front of it Kímolos, to the left of it Poliégos, on the right in the sea the block formed by Antimílos. But a monastery? None to be seen anywhere.

Only after proceeding along the difficult, gravelly path for some time do we see it down below. The trail gradually winds its way down through juniper bushes to the unoc-
1.55 cupied **monastery Panagía tósou neróu**, to the "Mother of God of the many waters"(see p. 41). A welcoming spot.
★ The church is plain and the rooms inviting: a long table and a kitchen with heaps of dishes (**P6:** N36°58.520'/ E24°40.283', 220m).

> **Bathing?** Right beside the monastery a few steps run down to a path which meanders on down through rocks. Turning right at a fork, you come to **Vlási pebble bay** [5] after a quarter of an hour.

1.55 From the forecourt of the monastery you stride down seven of the wide steps and then turn left into the terrain. Above the walled field trail "6" runs through a gully and then up through tall juniper bushes [6].
2.25 As a reward you have the fabulous **view** into the bays to come (**P7:** N36°58.160'/E24°40.787', 170m). Later the path is lined by walled fields and a round threshing floor (above left) (**P8:** N36°58.404'/E24°40.868').
2.45 The **chapel** of Constantine and his spouse Erini [7] is situated on an extensive terrace below the trail. Here in the middle of the nature reserve is a concentration of dramat-
2.55 ic rock formations. After a **spring** (**P9:** N36°57.986'/ E24°41.499', 395m) you climb up steps in the direction of the small white farmhouse on the hilltop.

Before reaching it, though, you come to the paved path,

3.05 which leads right to the **church Agía Marína** ⑧. Com-
★ pletely detached on top of a rock, it makes for a perfect resting place.
3.15 But now it is time to go up to the small **white house**, loudly guarded by several chained dogs (**P10:** N36° 57.780'/E24°41.790', 465m). Ten meters to the right of the house is a scarcely marked path to Katavatí – initially
3.20 it rather resembles an aisle leading through a **hollow.**
At first indistinct, later running between field walls, this path takes you along the edge of Mount Elias. At a broad open space you proceed to the left of the *passageway* (**P11:** N36°57,757'/E24°42,135', 465m). You then leave the wall on the right by going up left and at last rediscover a "6". Accompanied by a wall (right) it is now easier going as far as the paved path which leads up to the summit ⑮ (**P12:** N36°57.637'/E24°42.560', 380m).
4.00 Now it's a piece of cake: Hop down the path to the **bridge** (**P3:** N36°57.562'/E25°42.804', 250m), walk to the left and enjoy the twilight view of Katavatí. Cross the road at the information stand 20m to the right, take the concrete road through the dip and, up at the second fork, left. The main street in Katavatí leads to the loop in the road. Stroll proudly past the gymnasion (right) and down the alley
4.30 with steps to the **main square** of **Apollonía.** In the kafenion *Lakis* you can then tell everyone where you have just come from.

Kéa

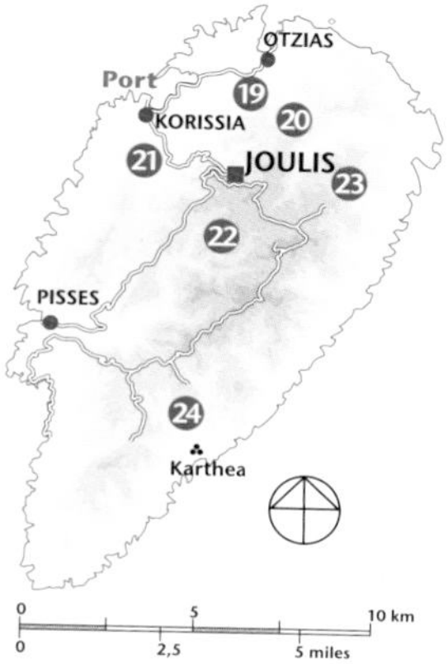

The second largest island in the West Cyclades, also known as "Zea", is one of the first islands to have been populated and was already an important trading centre with the Black Sea region in the 2nd millennium BC. The roof tiles on the houses do not correspond to the popular image of the Cyclades – rather indicating that it rains more often here. On account of its numerous springs and wells it possesses much thicker vegetation than the rest of the Cyclades – right into autumn indeed. The coastline, on the other hand, is rocky and inundated with sandy bays.
Groves of Walloon oaks and nut trees make it an ideal island for trekking, especially as the centre of the island still boasts many mule tracks which are also used.
The island administration encourages walking and has had 12 trails marked and cleared. The drawback is that some of these routes can only be covered with the aid of a taxi, as the bus timetable is not very hiker-friendly. Buses only run from June until August. Of all the walks described in this book, tours 21, 22 and 24 are to be recommended in particular.
Although Kéa can be reached from Athens airport within a couple of hours, international tourism has not yet arrived. In economically more propitious times the Athenians built a lot of holiday houses, but many of these have gone to rack and ruin since the financial crisis. The hospitality sector is rather underdeveloped, has a higher price level and tends to reach its limits on many a summer weekend. "Rooms" is a sign one hardly ever sees here.

Hiking maps: Anavasi #10.41 Terrain #301 (Tzia)
Taxis: +30- 6973 012813/ 6932 418821/ 6977 575888/ 6936 660251.
Hire cars should be reserved at weekends!
Leon 22880-21898, Stegadi -22651

⑲ Ioulís

The island's capital is the destination of this 3-hour trek. Apart from the well-liked cobbled path the route also uses roadways, which afford extensive views across the sea as well as the emblem of Kéa, the stone lion. The tour comes across a well.
■ 7 km, difference in altitude 180m, easy to moderate

AWT 0.00 Take a taxi for the 3 km to **Kómi.** About 30m beyond the little bridge, to the left of an electricity meter, begins the path marked "2". Initially it is a rather overgrown defile, but then it leads uphill on wonderful steps [1]. At the top you go to the right on a transversal roadway. Ioulís lies stretched out in the hills like an amphitheatre. On the left

0.10 of the roadway is the long **garden wall** of an enormous villa, before it leads over a crest. It runs almost evenly [2] past a right-hand turn-off and offers a fine view across the green coastal landscape, which is sprinkled with the white dots of several holiday houses. Out on the seabed somewhere lies the "Britannic", which hit a German mine in World War 1. The sister ship of the "Titanic", it served as a hospital ship.

0.20 At the **fork** you go right and, at a left-hand bend, strenuously uphill. But no more steep ascents after that! At the next fork the mountain ridge is crossed and you walk downhill again. To the left lie the bays of Voukári and Otziás with the holiday houses of the Athenians.

Having proceeded between the Prokopius Chapel and a villa (right), you need to continue a further 200m as far as a black water tank (right) and another 70m to where two

1

2

parts turn off to the right. There on the right stands an
0.45 electricity **distributor pole.**

> ***Shortcut:*** The path described below tends to be overgrown in places and hence the preserve of the true Cyclades hikers. The path marked "1" going left is a more comfortable way to the Benjamin well.

The persistent hiker sets off on the path going right; at first dropping abruptly, it later continues as a defile in the stream-bed. Where it is blocked by trees, it is necessary to detour this on the left.

Hanging on the right after about 10 minutes is a dilapi-
0.55 dated steel gate. 100m further comes the **turn-off** up to the left (**P1:** N37°38.940'/E24°20.858', 200m). After three minutes the somewhat overgrown monopáti brings you to the Tryfones Chapel. The path leads steeply uphill [3], then circumvents a farmhouse (left) and becomes a track
1.10 which soon reveals the large **Benjamin well.** Cattle markets used to be held on the large square with the gigantic plane tree in the middle.

Now we have almost reached our destination [4] – a wide
1.15 track takes us there, past the famous **lion** (down on the right, see p. 81). The well-used kalderími first runs past
1.20 the **cemetery** and then a church before arriving at **Ioulís.** A wide alley brings you safely back to the main square,
1.30 the **plateia.** All that is needed to complete the day is a free table with a view across the valley.

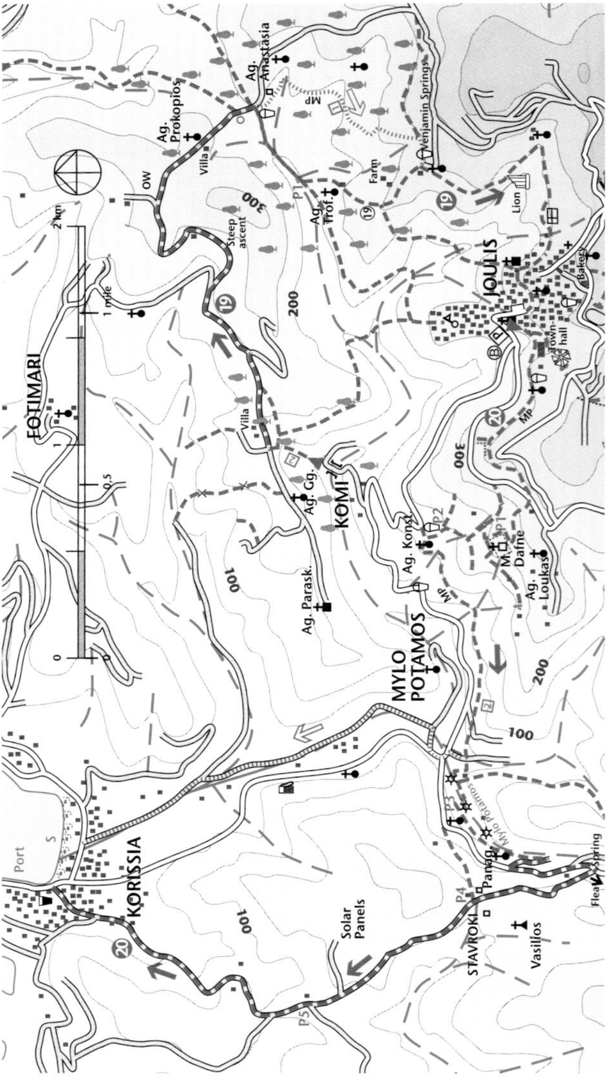

KORISSIA
Port
FOTIMARI
MYLO POTAMOS
KOMI
IOULIS
STAVROKL
Ag. Prokopios
Ag. Anastasia
Venjamin Springs
Ag. Trof.
Farm
Lion
Bakery
Town-hall
Ag. Gg.
Ag. Parask.
Ag. Konst.
M. Dafne
Ag. Loukas
Panag.
Vasilios
Flea Spring
Mylo Potamos
Solar Panels
Steep ascent
Villa
OW
MP
0
0.5
1
2 km
1 mile
100
200
300

⑳ The mill-stream

"Mylopótamos" means "mill-river". Actually it is more a stream, which used to serve 13 corn mills. It runs between Ioulís and Korissía, the end of this 3-hour trek along monopátia and kalderímia. Finally a dirt track leads across lonely heights.
■ 11 km, difference in altitude 310m, moderate

▷ *Map see left*

AWT
0.00 From the **bus stop in Ioulís** you climb up the steps to the right of the bank building. On the left you see a church after a few meters, on the right, on the other side of the valley, the classicist townhall, which you come below after having crossed a fork. That is where a path begins which affords a view of the wonderfully situated Ioulís. After the
0.05 bend comes a **well** on the left and a chapel.
Disregard the fork to the right in front of a wall with a door, continuing straight ahead on the splendid
0.15 monopáti as far as the **road.**
Directly opposite a gate opens onto the roadway which meanders down to the former Dafne nunnery [1] with
0.20 **threshing floor (P1:** N37°38.454'/E24°19.747', 270m). Going right to pass the enclosing wall, you come, 30m further down, to an indistinct, horizontal path heading right. After a turn to the right it comes, still before the vertical trench, to a somewhat overgrown path running downhill.
0.25 Further down you encounter a **mule track** which you follow to the right below a retaining wall. Stay on this level,

1

2

strolling along on the flat, until you come to a path which
joins from higher up; go left down it. Though not very
well kept, it leads between two little doors (**P2:** N37°
0.35 38.512′/E24°19.797′) to the **Constantine Chapel** ②.
This is where a wide paved track ③ marked "2" drops
0.50 down into the **valley** in broad sweeps. There we leave the
wide kalderími directly in front of the stream-bed *to the*
left and veer right after 30m, before the next house. Al-
ways keeping to the "2", we are led into a wild and ro-
mantic valley ④. We soon reach the first of the mills, a ru-
1.00 in, and traverse the **streamlet** two minutes later (**P3:**
N37°38.377′/E24°18.794′). In front of a renovated mill we
go right, then left immediately afterwards. There we see
two round hoppers with a diameter of one metre. This is
where the water was fed into the mill. By means of a slid-
ing valve at the bottom it was conducted on to a horizon-
tally running water-wheel, which operated the mill-
stones. It's long ago now ...
Next to the Panagía (Mother of God) chapel standing
above the right-hand side of the path we work our way up
1.05 right to the **road.** We march left uphill along this for about
120m as far as the sign "Xyla", which points up right.
Climbing gently, the dirt track leads to the deserted ham-
1.15 let of **Stavróki** (**P4:** N37°38.521′/E24°18.691′, 160m).
From there we head northwest and turn our backs on the
mill valley. What a contrast: the hilly landscape spread
out before us is largely barren and empty. For some time
we proceed above a valley down on the left and eventual-
1.35 ly reach a **holiday house** (right) at a fork (**P5:** N37°38.913′/
E24°18.334′). The next two forks do not deter us and we
1.55 arrive at the harbour in **Korissía** without further ado.

21 The smiling lion

The very impressive tour leads from Chóra to the bay of Otziás in about 3 hours. You walk beneath holm oaks as far as the chapel Agios Prokópios, after which you pass through a romantic gorge. The paths marked "1" are easy to follow and almost entirely downhill. Food and water can be dispensed with, but not bathing togs.
■ 7/13 km, , difference in altitude 290m, easy to moderate

AWT On the **main square** in Ioulís (290m) we take our leave of
0.00 the highly decorated war hero and parade uphill, use the
0.05 steps, pass a **church** (left) and, already outside the town, the cemetery (right). It is already possible to make out the symbol of the island. The trail is marked "1".

0.15 *Exactly why the **Lion of Kéa** 1 smiles in such an archaic way, and turns its back on the old town in a sulk, no-one knows. One thing is for sure: despite its great age of 2600 years, and its fragile body made of slate, it has kept in good shape. It is one of the oldest monumental sculptures in Greece.*

0.20 Our onward route soon passes the **Benjamin water-well** picturesquely arranged in a semi-circle round a plane tree. Major animal markets used to take place here, the metal rings serving to tether the animals. We continue in the same direction. The main track forks soon after the well
★ and along a kalderími 2 to the left you enter a quintessential Greek landscape with shady oak trees. After the hollow with narrow-leaved almond trees, you walk up

1

2

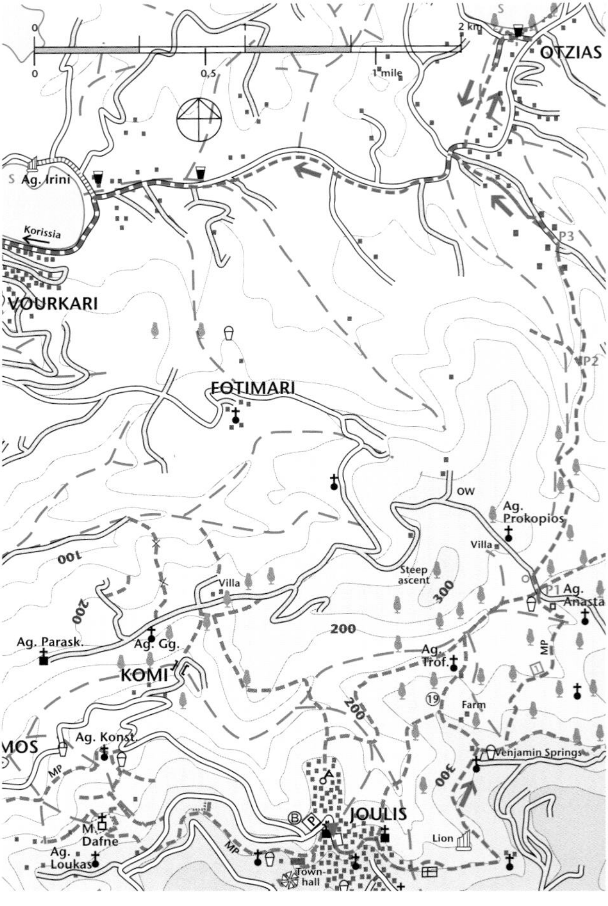

0.40 and come across a few **barns** with a cistern at a dirt road. (**P1:** N37°39.058′/E24°21.083′, 270m). Follow the road for 80m to the left and turn off to the right quite a way before the Agios Prokópios chapel and saunter along a monopáti running down through sparse woods and later into a dry-bed. Having passed bizarre

1.00 rock formations ③, you ignore the **left turn-off** of a path (**P2:** N37°39.592′/E24°21.210′) and follow the horizontal

panoramic route as far as a group of houses.

1.10 If you take the **dirt track** (**P3:** N37°39.922′/E24°21.136′) there for 40m to the left, you find a mule track leading down. The surrounding hills are gradually becoming covered with weekend cottages. The building regulations prescribe rough stone walls, in order to adapt to the landscape. Otziás is very popular with the Athenians, but they left numerous house ruins after 2008...

1.20 The roadway meets a **road.** 30m to the right of the bus shelter is another path which drops down to the **bathing**
1.25 **beach of Otziás** 4.

You can sit at the shady inn here while you wait for your taxi, should you be unable to tear yourself away.

Should you wish to proceed on foot, the road or the path to the left of it through the isthmus is the only choice. After half an hour you are again standing by the waterside, enjoying the view of Vourkári. You can stop at the taverna "Mimi" and bathe behind the Iríni peninsula.

*The **excavations on the Agía Iríni peninsula** are closed. You have to make do with peering through the fence.*

In the 1950s German archaeologists found four Bronze Age settlements which had existed here from 3000 BC until 1500 BC. Some of the artefacts are exhibited in the museum in Chóra.

Continuing past the tamarisk strand of Jaliskári and all manner of holiday architecture, it takes another half hour to get from here to **Korissía.**

22 The ancient road

The highlight of this hike is a 2500-year-old paved road through an oak grove, which the local people call "forest". Along fairy-tale mule and dirt tracks you traverse a deserted and densely vegetated area. 6 hours are sufficient for this very scenic circular tour. Along the way you will find a place to shop as well as a well. The route is initially marked "9", later "3".
■ 12 km, difference in altitude 240m, moderate to difficult

AWT Standing on the **platía in Ioulís** (290m) you can see the
0.00 large, rather concealed Dimitrios church looming above it. To reach the church, go up the main alley for a bit and take the first side-alley on the right after the bend. After 12 steps you pass a chapel (right). After 15m go left and immediately through a passageway. Next to a disused telephone box you come to a horizontal alley and go 30m
0.05 to the right. Then up further steps to the **church** of1883. With the church portal behind you, walk 30m on the same level to a long flight of steps and turn up left. 20m beyond an old marble well (right) further steps lead up to a large pine-tree (left). There a narrow roadway runs up
0.10 right, to the bakery (left) on the **road.** On the far side are signs and a dry well (**P1:** N37°38.251'/E24°20.501').
Take the path heading uphill towards "Myli", but then, after 100m, at the *fork* at the corner of the sports ground,
!! *go left.* After a wide expanse of rock you come to a little road in front of the Athanassis chapel (**P2:** N37°38.193'/

E24°20.587′, 450m). Turn left here, go uphill past two ruined windmills to the turn-off of a dirt track below a tall antenna.

Bear right here. Lined up on the right-hand side are the
0.20 windmills. The path runs **below holiday houses** (left) and then to the left of a farmhouse. Soon we reach the
0.25 double chapel of **Agios Ioánnis & Theologos** 1. It is tawdrily furnished, but offers a quiet spot to sit in front. 50m further on you turn off to the left in front of a stone hut (**P3:** N37°37.820′/E24°20.599′, 475m) and march down into the valley in the direction of the unspeakable antennae. Later down to the left the St. George's chapel 2 can be discerned in the valley.

50m after the left turn-off to George's chapel stands a new
0.40 **chapel** with a spectacular place to rest on the left (**P4:** N37°37.416′/E24°20.730′). Here you turn left to lovely descending steps. Once down on the valley bottom, you first wander to the right, then continue along the dry stream-bed for about seven minutes. Disregard the forest path going left. Having emerged from the trees, you
0.50 saunter left up **a path on slabs of rock** (**P5:** N37°37.416′/E24°20.730′). Up on the left stands a chapel.

Ignore the wider path leading down into the valley, instead continuing along above it until the monopáti 3
1.05 sadly ends near the **St. Nicholas chapel** (left) and two houses (**P6:** N37°36.920′/24°20.512′, 485m).

That is where a dirt track to the left begins, from which the signposted trail "9" soon branches off to the right, but that is of no concern to us. We allow ourselves to be led by the pleasant dirt track first on the flat, then uphill to the
1.30 **road** (**P7:** N37°36.750′/E24°21.230′). Under its asphalt

lies the ancient flagstone track.

There we trek towards the antennae for eight minutes, turning off to the left after a few
!! houses (left), *vis-à-vis a wayside altar* on to the wide old flagstone road. (**P8:** N37°37.058'/ E24°21.370'). This ancient road was constructed to connect the ancient towns of Ioulís and Karthéa ㉔. It is marked "3".

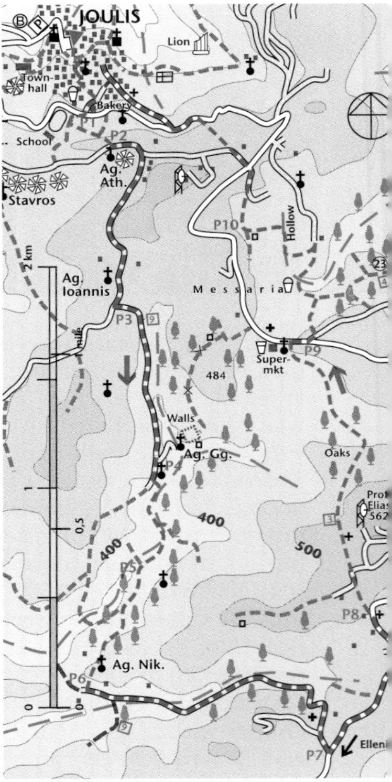

The trail runs further up on a dirt track, but which then swings off to the right. At the highest point (515m) stands a wayside altar, where you continue straight on and then descend the worn
★ steps ④. Old oak trees provide welcome shade. After a hollow you come up to the
2.05 **road.** (For those who are thirsty: supermarket on the left!) You go 80m to the right up the road, turning left at the sign "Episkopí" (**P9:** N37°37.732'/E24°21.165') and 20m after that left again on to a mule track. (Those who wish to take a look at the abandoned fortified monastery of Episkopí stay on the dirt track (see p. 88). Further along the shady mule track you turn off to the left and come to
2.10 a large **well.**

From here you follow a right-hand bend across the valley bottom and uphill on graceful steps. Then you must watch out: 30m before the first house on the right you
!! have to *turn off left* in the reverse direction. A somewhat
2.15 overgrown **monopáti** takes you over a crest and, in the dip which follows, to the right. Thanks to the first hikers

in spring, who have trampled down the tall thistles over a distance of some 20m, you hurtle happily left up to an abandoned house (left).

2.25 At the **fork** there (**P10:** N37°37.991'/E24°20.983') you turn off right, come to a little road and go left. On the
2.30 other side of the following **crossing** you continue for 120m on the dirt track (direction "mills") and then go right on to a mule track, from where it is soon possible to
2.35 see Ioulís. Having crossed the **road** to the left, you stride along the ramp towards **Ioulís** and arrive – either via vari-
2.45 ous alleys or more or less directly – at the **platía.**

Rural Chapels

They are everywhere along the way, the small chapels which characterise the image of the Greek countryside. They are usually owned by farmers. The room's ceiling is either covered with flat beams or vaulted with barrel-vaults of masonry. Larger churches have a dome above a cruciform ground plan; these are called "cruciform-domed churches".

In front, a lovingly cared-for spot with a bench and often, in a tree, a bell. This is where the consecration of the church, the "Panigíri", is celebrated with singing and dancing every year on the anniversary of the church's patron saint. The relatives come from far and wide, bringing delicacies for everyone. Sometimes the hiker is lucky to turn up at the right moment. Inside, the altar wall is opposite the door, the iconostasis made of lacquered wood with icons in the compartments. The representation of the patron saint is to the right of the passage. The room behind this one is called the "Bema" and should only be entered by the priest.

㉓ Beneath oaks ...

... is where this almost 6-hour, very beautiful trek begins, heading to the sea through sparsely populated, broad hillsides. Mostly on cobbled paths and past two springs, the tour does however require twice overcoming considerable differences in altitude.
■ 16 km, difference in altitude 480m, difficult

AWT Take a hire car or taxi along the road above Ioulís and turn into the country road leading south. 5 km beyond Chóra, to the left of the road, stands the signpost EPISKOPI (**P1:** N37°37.732'/E24°21.165').

0.00 Leave the car at the **dustbin site** and march inland along the lane. After three minutes, in the dip - 70m before the monastery -, turn left on to a path [1].

*The abandoned **fortified monastery of Episkopí** is a picturesque complex on ancient ground. The stone tower must have been a Hellenistic observation point. The capital of a Doric column forms the lower part of the altar in the church.*

Beneath oaks the narrow, rather overgrown path leads to
0.05 a **T-junction**, where you go right. Also *disregard* the left-hand turn-off after three minutes (**P2:** N37°37.895'/E24°21.347', 440 m). Continue on the same level, partly on a terrace, then on steps and turn left at a lattice door. Only a few olive trees are to be seen, the scenery being dominated by oak trees. After a dwelling (left) the path is
0.15 easier to discern [2]. On cobbles it leads down to a **concrete track** and then into a hamlet. Here you drop 150m as far as the last houses (**P3:** N 37°37.905'/E 24°21.694').

1

2

!! Caution – here our cobbled path runs *left* down into the green valley, where a path branches
0.20 off left to the **Sotíras spring** (**P4:** N37°37.987′/E24°21.736′, 380m).
From there elegant stone steps take you uphill beneath oaks (p. 124) and back out into the open. A
0.30 **level section** of the trail (**P5:** N37°38.148′/E24°21.950′, 430m) offers fine views across the hilly and sparsely populated west side of Kéa.
After encountering a
0.35 **roadway,** you turn off left and, after 100m, right on the same level. At a yard for construction
0.40 steel you cross the **road** diagonally to the right.
At a cistern (**P6:** N37°37.910′/E24°22.230′, 450m) a wonderful cobbled path starts in the direction of the sea 3, later running past a derelict house. Beyond the gate,
!! which opens on the *left,* you again re-enter wide open countryside. Proceed to the right of the long wall, following it
1.00 down *left* to a **wall-corner** (**P7:** N37°37.791′/E24°22.796′, 340 m).

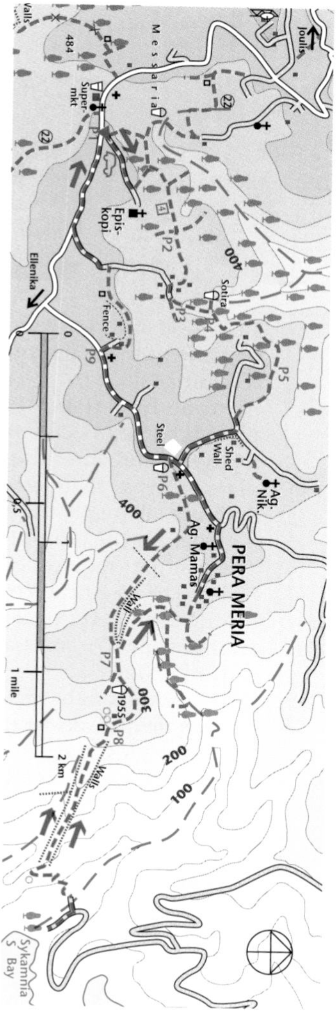

Turn to the right on the path which comes there from the left and, shortly afterwards, walk horizontally to the left at a fork. This initially leads across a rock before levelling
1.05 out and then down steps to the **well of 1995.** There the

3

4

steps lead up to a panorama trail, from where it is also possible to make out our destination, a sandy bay with a few tamarisks.

1.15 At **stone huts** (**P8:** N37°37.746'/E24°23.088', 270m) the path, accompanied by walls, swings down to the sea [4]. At a large round threshing floor it turns left to the coastal
1.45 plain. On a roadway you reach the **sandy bay of Sikamía.** Beneath the tamarisks you can recharge your batteries for the return leg.

The first part requires quite a lot of energy in order to get back up to an altitude of 270m to **P8.** There you continue
2.10 on the same level to the **well of 1995** and on up to the
2.15 **wall-corner P7.** You have overcome a difference in altitude of 340m!

Here you walk right, first on the same level, then climbing
2.25 steps beneath oaks to the hamlet **Péra Meriá/Ágios Mamas.** Not a lot to see, though – so press on! Going along a lane you reach the road, where you go up left at the wayside altar.

2.40 At the **yard for steel** you stay on the road and proceed to-
2.50 wards the antennas, until where you find a **wayside altar** on the right (**P9:** N37°37.748'/E24°21.867'). There you turn off right on to a lane and after 30m, to the right of the fence, you stalk along a partly visible trail as far as a stone hut. Behind this a monopáti leads right to a road-
3.05 way. Walking left up it, you return to the **road** and con-
3.10 tinue right to the **signpost to Episkopí.** Those who eschew the hire car and taxi can get to Ioulís on foot by following the description on page 86. AWT 2.35.

24 The temples of Karthéa

A path cobbled with marble 2500 years ago leads down to the remains of the ancient city of Karthéa. The round trip takes 4 hours – or a little longer for those interested in archaeology. It is necessary to take provisions with you, for the route offers neither springs nor eateries. And a hire car is required to get to the starting point and back.
■ 8 km, difference in altitude 360m, moderate

AWT Arriving from Ioulís, you drive past **Ellenika** and, 900m beyond it, turned off left at the **sign "Ag. Symeon".** After two kilometres, in front of a white wayside altar, you proceed to the right. Rising up on the cone-shaped mountain to the left is the clearly visible Simon's monastery. Park the car next to a large farmstead (left) beyond some holiday villas.

0.00 Walking down the **rural lane** which commences there, you descend a little more steeply after a wayside altar (right) and pass the Athanassios chapel (left) [1]. From the
0.05 **start of the footpath** between two metal gates you are accompanied by tiny red-and-white metal signs ("4").
After a droll wayside altar – a minuscule church – the path
0.15 **forks** [2]. You go *straight ahead,* although the trail is more
!! overgrown (**P1:** N37°34.531'/E24°20.145'). On the right is a deep valley, which also leads to Karthéa. Having strolled along above terraces [3], you see the tour's destination after a bend – first the Panagía chapel, then the plateau of the Athena Temple above the sea [4].
0.30 Time to celebrate the magnificent view at the **picnic area**

1

2

★ on a lump of rock (**P2:** N37°33.998′/E24°19.927′, 140m) – provided you have remembered to bring along the drinks. Further down the path is slightly more difficult to find.
0.45 After a metal gate (left) keep left on the green **coastal plain.** 30m before the beach turn right and climb up to
0.50 the **Temples of Karthéa.**

Since 1811 two temples have been excavated on two plateaus and they were restored in 2009. The lower plateau belongs to the Temple of Apollon Pythios, the upper one, situated on a cyclopean wall, Athena. The construction period was from 500 to 300 BC. On the other side of the temples are a chapel and the archaeologists' shed.

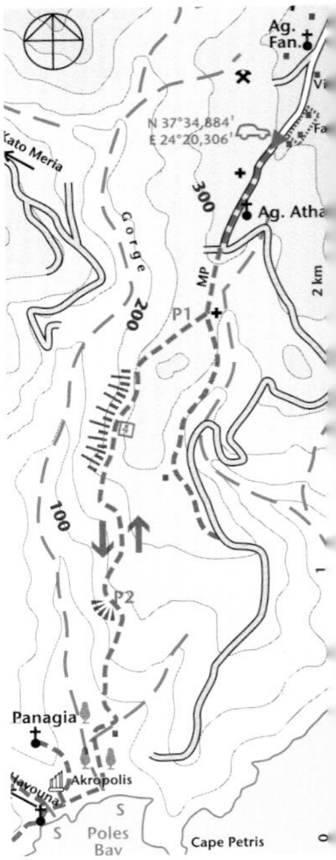

0.50 From the green **coastal plain** you go back up the same path. If you use the white stone house up on the right as your marker, you cannot go wrong. After the right-
1.30 hand bend you again **see** the Simon's monastery and arrive back
1.45 at the **car.** (Hopefully you have not lost the key while bathing.)

Anáfi

The most south-easterly island of the Cyclades is isolated and mountainous. Like Santorini Anáfi lies on the South Aegean Volcanic Arc and suffered just as devastating damage in the earthquake of 1956.
The almost treeless island is hardly used for agriculture apart from sporadic patches of vegetation in valleys and sheltered hollows. The isolated island remained largely uninhabited for some 200 years due to marauding pirates and even today is barely cultivated. Hence only simple mule tracks without walls are to be found.
Although it possesses wonderful beaches, the island is still off the beaten track as far as mass tourism goes. To sit up in Chóra is a gift with which only very few are endowed. Anáfi is certainly worth the two-hour crossing from Santorini.
Hiking maps: Nakas-Road # 115 Terrain # 318
No taxis, island bus from June. Tel. for emergencies: 0030-22860 61266.

25 The green heart

Like many Greek islands, Anáfi appears to be rugged and rocky from the sea. Yet in the middle are green valleys – at least in spring. The 2-hour circular tour takes us through hilly countryside, partly on old paths. Along the way, though, we encounter neither tavernas nor wells.
■ ***6.5 km, difference in altitude 140 m, easy***

AWT At the bus parking place in **Chóra** you turn off the main
0.00 road to the left beside the quaint chapel and the antenna and then pass two windmills (left). This is where an old mule track begins, running north along the edge of the slope [1]. After a bend you see the helicopter pad up on the top of the mountain.

0.12 Besides house ruins you come to a wide **dirt track** (**P1:** N36°21.523'/25°46.344', 305m). (This is where the pathless short cut of tour 26 begins). You go left here and soon
0.20 reach the few houses of **Psáthi**, above which towers a chapel on the right. Take a final glance back at the fantastically situated Chóra, stretching out above the sea. After three minutes the dirt track winds sharply to the right, but following the remains of the old mule track you go
0.30 *straight* ahead, climbing slowly until you rejoin the **dirt track** at a power line (**P2:** N36°21.925'/E25°45.992', 360m).
0.35 Now go left as far as a **holiday house** built of rubble masonry. The (fake) windmill standing above it makes a good place to rest.

At the holiday house you continue in the same direction *on the upper track,* go round the hill and soon see the Stavrós chapel standing below Mount Vígla [2].

Before you get there is a cross-roads (cross = Greek "stavrós") (**P3:** N36°22.213'/E25°45.875', 345m), where until a few years ago several mule tracks converged.

Hiking to the right or south-east on a dirt track, then
0.45 above some **chapels** standing on the left in the valley,
★ you appreciate the panoramic view across the island's green heartland, with its patchwork of fields, chapels and little houses. At the end of the dirt track begins a narrow path (**P4:** N36°22.039'/E25°46.043') which later affords

1

2

even better views over as far as Mount Kálamos. This path runs above a wide valley and brings you back to the already familiar
1.00 **dirt track** near Psáthi. Go left along it and leave it again later before it ascends by going right on to the also familiar path below the helipad (**P1**). This leads
1.15 back to **Chóra.**

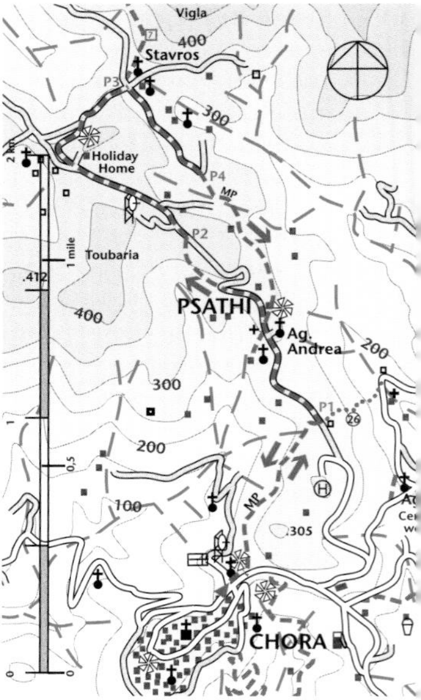

▶ From **Chóra** to the **beach of Klissióni.** A trail leads from the last guest-house at the end of the village, below the road, to two chapels and then down the hill opposite Chóra to the road. After a short stretch you reach the road leading to Klissióni.

▶ To reach **Katsoúni beach**, follow the road to the port for about 500 m and, at the signs to Kastélli, turn left on to a path, then right again downhill.

26 The dream beach

This 6-hour circular walk leads through hills below the remains of the ancient town of Anáphe and then on down to the sandy beach of Roúkonas, where you can stop at a taverna and might possibly get the bus. You return to Chóra along narrow paths above the coast. Water and perhaps food should be taken along, as the beach taverna is only open in season.
■ 13 km, difference in altitude 280m, moderate to difficult

AWT ***Short cut:*** Those who do not mind pathless hiking could take the route of **tour 25 as far as P1**, go straight across the roadway and descend into the valley below. The best place to cross the road is at the water culvert in the ditch.

0.00 From **Chóra** you take the road leading down to the port and turn up left after about 350m at a house with large retaining walls. After 3 min. you bear down right in the direction of the gravel works. On the crest above this plant a narrow defile cuts off the bend in the road to the left.
0.15 Passing the **St. George's double chapel** (right) (**P1:** N36° 21.354'/E24°46.562', 200m) you come, again on the road, to a culvert (see short cut) and a house ruin. Walking round the valley full of cactus plants, you leave the as-
0.25 phalt at a power line with sign by going right on to a **dirt track** (**P2:** N36°21.572'/E25°46.663', 160m).
Proceed down the dirt track until you find a path in a trough (**P3:** N36°21.570'/E25°46.739'). Walk up it be-
0.30 tween two **house ruins** 1. After two minutes the path

veers right, climbing along the right of the hill. After a small saddle with olive trees and ruined houses down on the right you see a green hollow and above, a wide moun-
0.45 tain ridge. On the left of it you reach a **saddle** ② along trails (**P4:** N36°21.656′/E25°47.313′, 235m).
Above the next valley is Kastélli mountain, to the right of whose peak once lay the Dorian town of Anáphe. We meander down along mountain trails, first left, then right to the baking-oven and from there zig-zag to the intersection between two valleys marked by a barn and a small farmhouse in a garden.
1.00 Below the house you traverse the reed-covered **valley floor** (Kálista) and, further up on the opposite slope, find the continuation of the trail. The path runs past some ru-
1.25 ins and a barn up a slight incline to the **Chapel of Dokári Panagía** (**P5:** N36°21.313′/E25°47.914′). In front of it a well-preserved sarcophagus has found its present resting place, very likely having been put to use as a cattle-trough. Griffons, the horse Pegasus and six Cupids are depicted.

From here one could scramble up to the ruins of the ancient town of Anáphe in 10 minutes. See ㉗.

On account of the steep slopes the route first heads to-

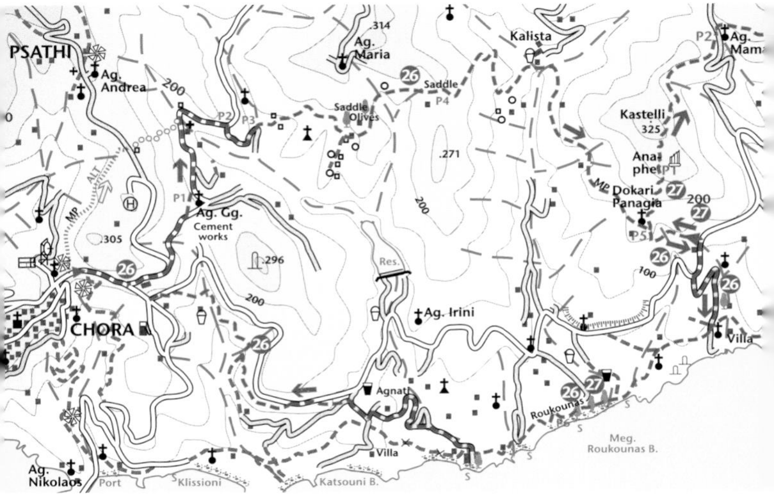

wards Mount Kálamos. You have to pound the asphalt on
1.35 the **road** for 200m until, on the left, you find where a
roadway turns off. Further down a path turns off this to
★ the right. It runs down past a chapel to the dream beach
1.55 of **Roúkonas**. The taverna is open from June. Bus connec-
tions should be established beforehand!
At the western end of the long strand, in the dry valley
(**P6:** N36°20.828'/E25°47.661') paths begin, running
above the coast and skirting two bays. At the second of
these, a coarse gravel bay with an elongated house, it is
2.10 best to go up the **roadway**, for the paths across the hill are
all obstructed further up.
2.30 Up at the **fork** below the road (right Café Agnati) you go
left along the wide path and then, after 80m, after the
walls, right along a narrow path which is later interrupted
by roadworks. So you have to climb up to the road, but al-
ready after 100m you can return to the path running par-
3.00 allel below and saunter carefree on to **Chóra.**

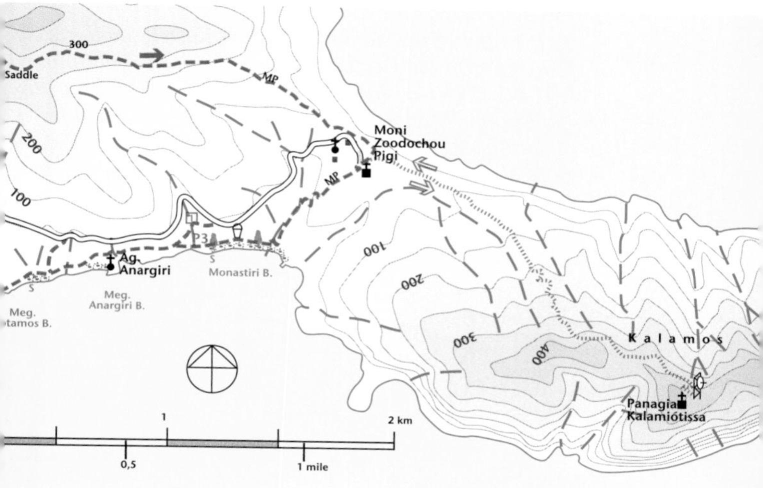

27 Kálamos marble cliffs

What is probably the finest tour on Anáfi takes at least 5 hours. Almost entirely on paths, you skirt the ruins of the ancient town of Anáphe, the "lower" monastery Zoodóchos Pigís and end up at the sandy beach of Roukónas.
The huge marble Mount Kálamos watches over the hiker the whole time. It would be possible to visit the "upper monastery" on it too – but then better take the bus part of the way!
One could also substitute the approach to the "Kastelli" mentioned below with walk 26.
■ 10 km, difference in altitude 235 m, moderate to difficult

▷ *Map see previous pages*

AWT Either by bus or with the help of your hotelier you drive along Roukónas beach and up past a double vaulted
0.00 house (left). The walk commences at **paved steps** and the "Kastelli" sign (left).
0.06 A path leads up to the **chapel Panagía Dokári** (p. 98). To
0.20 the right of it the path continues up to **Anáphe (P1: N36°21.525'/E25°47.971', 235m).**

To the right of the summit of Mount Kastelli lie the cyclopean walls of the **Dorian town of Anáphe,** *built around 800 BC. The remains of the buildings still make a huge impression. The town was abandoned after Roman times, about 500 AD, probably because of an earthquake. At the time a processional road led from here to the temple of*

1

2

Apollo in Kálamos. That is the way we want to go today. Up to 1998 exquisite marble statues from the Roman period were found on the site. They were partly damaged in a clearance fire and are now on display at the museum in Chóra.

Past a small, ancient water basin (left), you gradually descend the right-hand side of Mount Kastelli. Your first goal is a small chapel ①. Your ultimate goal, a large monastery, is still hidden at the foot of the mighty Mount Kálamos on the right. Initially you walk downhill on the right-hand side of a wall, soon on the same level, then in sharp hairpin bends. Later leisurely round a valley and
0.35 the opposite slope to the **chapel Ágios Mámas (P2:** N36°21.819'/E25°48.129', 230m). Directly behind it the continuation runs almost horizontally along the edge of the mountain.

0.55 On the **ridge** Kálamos comes into view with every step. A
★ magnificent picture. The two white monasteries above and below can now be clearly seen. When descending ② you can make out the path rising to the upper monastery. Our scree path, rather strenuous at this point, leads us to
1.30 the **"lower monastery"** ③.

The abandoned ***Monastery of Zoodóchos Pigís,*** *the "life-giving source", is 200 years old and was built on and from the ancient ruins of an Apollo temple. Ancient recycling, the archaeologist's nightmare. This temple has its origins in the realm of Greek legend. The Argonauts, who stole the Golden Fleece from the "Eldorado" of Colchis on the east coast of the Black Sea, first set foot on Greek land again here after a stormy sea journey and, out of gratitude, set up an altar on this site which subsequently became a temple.*

In summer the monastery is open to visitors until 1.00 pm.
The more than three-hour excursion to the summit first leads past the new picnic spot and then becomes an easily identifiable rocky path up the mountain ridge. A good head for heights is essential at the top, as steep inclines have to be overcome before we can finally enjoy the view from the summit, from **Panagía Kalamiótissa,** the patron saint of the island.

Over the past 400 years several churches have been built on this spot. The present one was rebuilt in 1956, having been destroyed during the immense earthquake. Monks are also supposed to have lived here earlier. Up until a bad accident caused by lightning more than 100 years ago, the Anáphians used to trek up here for the church celebrations each year! Nowadays they only drive to the monastery on the mountain below.

1.30 Going right from the picnic spot at the lower monastery, past two column drums, it takes 12 minutes to drop down to the beach, where tamarisks provide shade ④. At the second clump of trees, after the tongue of rock, a path (**P3:** N36°21.293'/E25°49.421') leads through low undergrowth across the cliffs and joins the wide coastal path
1.55 "1". First this passes the **Anárgiri chapel,** then three sandy coves. At the third one, Mégalo Potamós, you leave the ruts as soon as they start!

For a while the path then climbs, leaving the sea and, in a
2.20 damp valley, runs round a **holiday home** with tacky "windmill". Further up the path forks behind white boundary posts. We descend left on green schist and
2.30 come to a small **chapel,** which comprises parts of ancient structures. On the coastal plateau are head-high stone towers. Similar ones served as markers for the former Anáphe harbour.

From the chapel you use goat tracks down to the sandy
2.35 beach of **Roúkonas.** This offers an inn in summer and the bus in to Chóra.

If you want/have to hoof it there (+ 65 min. AWT) the description on page 99 can help.

Folégandros

The Chóra (see below) is certainly one of the most beautiful places in the Cyclades, with a kástro and tiny squares.
The eastern part of the island is scarcely farmed. In the western part on the other hand the agricultural terraces continue to be tilled. That is where marked mule tracks can still be found.
Hiking maps: Terrain # 316
The taxi: +30-69446-93957

28 The west coast

Away in the west lies a beautiful bay which is only accessible on foot or by bathing boat. It takes 4 hours to reach plus another hour up to Ano Meriá, from where the bus heads back to Chóra. Be sure to obtain the bus timetable before setting out.
It is also possible to take the boat back from Livadáki beach to Angáli. The very beautiful walk exclusively follows mule tracks, but does not offer anywhere to stop, only a well. A short cut would be to take the bus to Angáli.
■ 11 km, difference in altitude 260 m, difficult

▷ *Map see page 108*

AWT As far as Stavrós Chapel the beginning of the trek is identical with walk ㉙.
0.15 20m beyond the **Stavrós Chapel**, with a bounce in your

step, you saunter right on to a roadway which soon leads
0.20 past three **windmills** 1. Immediately after the third one you drop right and at once left. The narrow path runs daringly along the steep coastline until you once more come
0.30 up to the Saranda chapel on the **road.**

Go down this road to the left for 80m, leaving it again to the right 30m after Paraskévi chapel (right) (**P1:** N36° 37.993'/E24°54.172', 155m). An old path marked "AL" leads down into Angáli valley. From the wall-lined path you can soon pick out the buildings on the bay. Having passed a couple of houses to the right of the path, you
0.50 cross a concrete road near two **wells.** (You can draw water from the upper well.)

Diagonally opposite, 15m further up to the right and somewhat concealed, are a few steps leading on uphill (**P2:** N36°38.153'/E24°53.726'). Our mule track runs along the side of the slope, Angáli on the left. (On the right a steep path soon leads up to Ano Meriá.) We wander on ef-
0.55 fortlessly, following the contour lines. In a **dry-bed** (**P3:**
!! N36°38.133'/E24°53.490') we go *straight* (not left) uphill! First on the rocks in the dry-bed, then leisurely on a path
1.00 going left we arrive at the abandoned hamlet **Georgi t'Aga**, with three palm-trees. 50m beyond the hamlet a path branches off up to Ano Meriá ㉙ – here too we go straight ahead, but down left after 80m at a fork (**P4:** N36°38.068'/ E24°53.332', 110m).

Walking along above the coastline on tour 29 in the opposite direction, you notice the holiday lets on Galifos bay which, with their paraffin lamps in the evenings, still promise true romanticism. Later you look down on Agios Nikoláos bay with the tamarisks.

The descending track becomes narrower – in the course of
the years it has been trodden into the slate. 60m before
1.10 the ruins of the hamlet Mármaro at a triangular **fork** (P3
from ㉙) the path turns off left to Agios Nikoláos bay. We
wander up right, through Mármaro and drop down into a
hollow ③, above which a Stavros chapel stands watch. Be-
1.15 low us rather murky **water** gathers in a **pool**, albeit in a
bed of noble marble.
Regrettably the route climbs yet again, and rather strenu-
ously too – on a path across eroded rock. Afterwards it
crosses a strung-out olive grove, which rises up the moun-
1.30 tain in a **hollow.** This is where the path ends (**P5:** N35°
38.088′/E24°52.743′).
On the left of the ascending wall, the shortest link to the
summit, you follow the blue and "FL" markings upwards
to the right. Where the walls narrow again, the path forks
1.40 **above a house** (left). The plateau is farmed in enclosed
fields. Our route leads left between these towards the sea.
When you reach the hill shortly afterwards, bear right
and slowly downhill. Hugging the hillside, the track turns
right before a field wall. The lighthouse comes into view,
beyond it Mílos. Following the wall on the left-hand side,
2.00 you come to **ruined houses** (**P6:** N36°38.026′/E24°51.881′,
110m), where you continue right and uphill again.
Still with the wall immediately to the left, the path takes a
broad sweep round the lighthouse, which soon lies on the
port side abeam. Behind the wall be sure to observe the
blue dots and cairns! The track descends to the bay on the
right through rocks in several bends. The final stretch
2.25 runs horizontally on a rocky path to **Livadáki Bay** ③ (**P7:**
N36°38.160′/E24°51.547′). Beneath tamarisks one can

now enjoy the sun and the sea and perhaps take the kaiki back (last sailing 5 pm).

On the other side of the bay, beside a stone hut, a wide path leads uphill. If you look back from there, you can catch another glimpse of the lighthouse and the dramatic rocky coastline. The easily identifiable path (LV) ends at another stone hut (left) in front of walls and merges with
2.40 a **monopáti** at a gap (**P8:** N36°38.026'/E24°51.882').
This monopáti leads uphill [4], past the ruins of a hamlet
3.05 (left) and as far as the closed **summit chapel Anargíri.** It offers spectacular panoramic views of Poliégos and Mílos. The mule track continues on up to the road leading to the
3.25 right to **Ano Meriá-Agios Andréas.** In the village you walk past the bus turning place to the inn *The Meeting-place* (**P9:** N36°38.881'/E24°52.146'). That is the best place to test whether the bus is punctual.

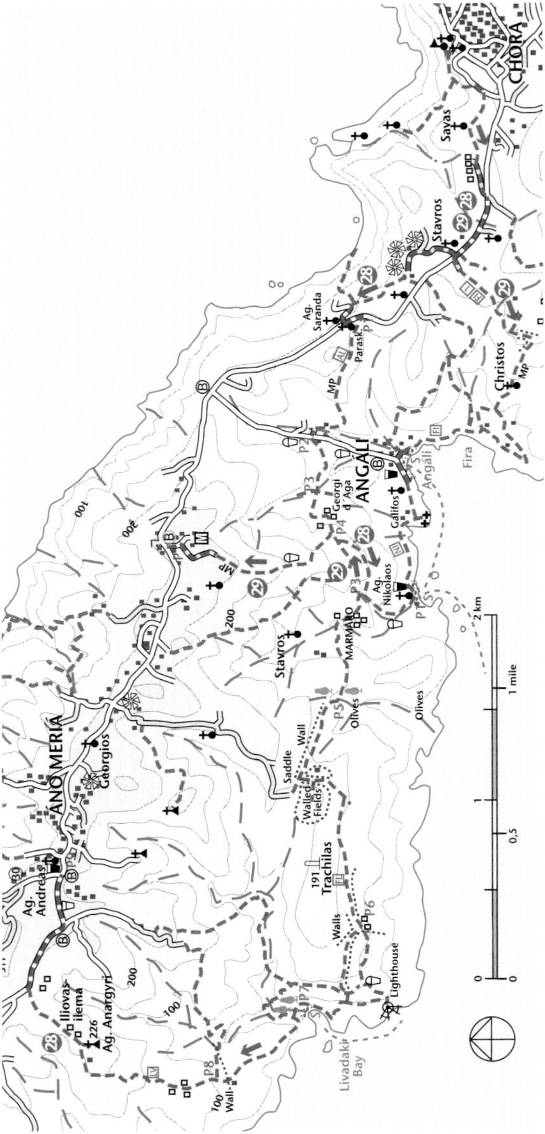
CHORA
Sayas
Stavros
Ag. Saranda
Parask.
Christos
MP
Fira
Angali
ANGALI
Georgi d' Aga
Galifos
Ag. Nikolaos
MARMARO
Stavros
Olives
Olives
Saddle
Wall
Walled Fields
191
Trachilas
Walls
Lighthouse
Livadaki Bay
Wall
ANO MERIA
Georgios
Ag. Andreas
Iliovas-ilema
226
Ag. Anargyri
100
200
0
0,5
1
1 mile
2 km

㉙ Angáli bay

This 4-hour walk leads, entirely along paths, to the two finest sandy beaches with shady tavernas. It ends up in Ano Meriá.
■ 7 km, difference in altitude 280 m, moderate

▷ *Map see left*

AWT To the left of the tavern "Araxe" on the main square, with
the large tree behind you, stroll into the alley, then left at
the fish tavern and leave the **Chóra** on a descending con-
0.00 crete ramp. Below the edge of Chóra a **footpath** [1] makes
its way high above the sea and the terraces, and below the
road. Always following the contour lines, it passes the
0.05 flat-roofed **Sávas chapel** (right) in the saddle. Beyond the
following hollow, beside unfinished buildings, begins a
0.10 dirt track which, at a sharp angle, comes to the **road**,
along which we proceed to the right for 300m. *20m after*
0.15 the **Stavrós chapel** (above right) you turn off left on to
the track higher up, which later becomes a path.
0.20 With a wall on the left, it leads to a **hollow** [2], (**P1:**
N36°37.581'/E24°54.172', 155m) with the only farm-
house in the area. The paved trail marked "Fira" leads up
again and is then walled on both sides. When the walls
0.25 **drift apart**, we follow the one on the right downhill in a
wide arc. Then comes a big surprise: a kalderími paved
with multicoloured marble slabs runs through this moun-
★ tainous area. An olive grove comes into view above the
sea and this enchanting Cycladic picture is complement-
0.30 ed by the **Christos chapel** [3].

150m below the chapel, at the fence, turn off right on to a path leading to the shed further down. Below the house
0.40 on the right is the stony **Firá bay.** From here you reach
0.50 the sandy beach of **Angáli** along small paths through boulders. During the season a taverna awaits you.

A ramp and concrete steps lead up from the beach to a coastal path. Past two altars (left) and the guest house in Galifos it brings you to the tamarisk-covered sandy bay of
1.10 **Agios Nikoláos** (**P2:** N36°37.825'/E24°53.075'). Overlooking it is a panoramic café, while the fine sandy beach later offers shady trees.

After a well-earned rest we go through a gap in the wall *15m behind* the beach bar's power generator, then immediately uphill on a well-beaten track (blue dots). Later the walls narrow in an incision coming from the left, leading us uphill on to a monopáti. Further up, to the right of the
1.20 ruins of Marmaro, this merges with a **mule track** which runs along the side of the slope (**P3:** N36°37.583'/E24°54.172'). If you follow it to the right, you come after a while to another fork, where you go down to the right. 80m before the ruins of the hamlet **Georgi t'Aga** (with
1.30 palms) you go left at a **turn-off** and, strenuously, but with a fabulous view 4, rather steeply uphill. At the top you come to the Museum of Ethnology (open from 5 pm) (**P4:** N36°38.503'/E24°53.170'). To the right we reach the road
2.00 and the bus stop of **Áno Meriá.**

30 The terraces of Fournídes

The 3-hour hike takes in the fertile farmland in the north, where many monopatía are still preserved and actually used too. The only shady trees are to be found on the pebble beach of Ágios Geórgios and places to stop for refreshments at the end of the marvellous tour.

■ 6.5 km, difference in altitude 260m, easy to moderate

AWT In **Ágios Andréas**, the northern part of the street village
Ano Meriá, the tour starts on a concrete track on the left-
0.00 hand side of the **taverna** "ΣUVÁVTNON" ("the meeting
place"). Follow this to the cluster of houses on a hilltop,
where you walk downhill, bearing right at a fork. A sum-
mit chapel [1] may later be spotted on the right above the
track.

On the left below this chapel, Ágios Sóstis, you ramble
0.10 straight on down at a large **triangular junction** (**P1:** N36°
39.277'/E24°51.957', 215 m). From the kalderími you
soon see the fishermen's houses at the destination [2]. On
the left numerous grain terraces cover the hills of this re-
gion, which is called **Fournídes.**
0.20 At a **T-junction** you go left (**P2:** N36°39.617'/E24°51.972'),
passing a right-hand turn-off after two minutes. The path
0.30 joins a **roadway**, which brings you to the **pebble bay of**
0.35 **Ágios Geórgios.** Surrounded by rocks, the bay has a few
tamarisks for the comfort of the mostly motorised
bathers.

The way back takes you inland along the level roadway

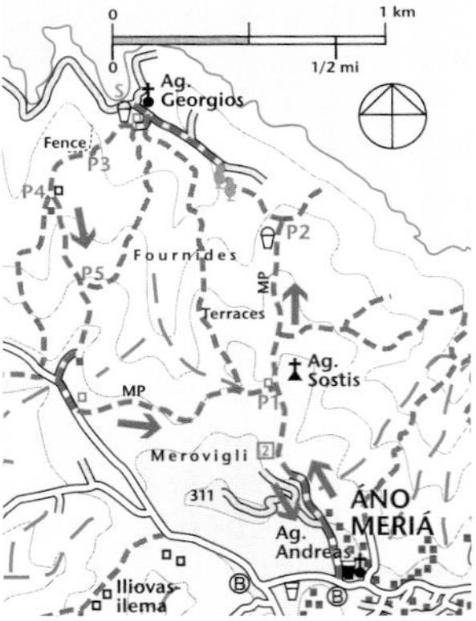

and then right to a well (right). Two paths begin there – we choose the ascending one. It runs directly uphill, where it curves left in front of a fence (**P3:** N36°39.760′/ E24°51.504′, 70 m). The path then continues more or less evenly
0.50 ③. After a **fork** at a house ruin (left) (**P4:** N36°39.666′/ E24°51.413′) you climb left, now more steeply again ④. Another path coming from the bay merges from the left (**P5:** N36°39.486′/E24° 51.472′, 175 m). Next to a shed (left) is a track leading to
1.05 the **road**, which you ascend to the left.
After 100m, to the right of a cistern, a level path begins on
1.20 the left, which guides you delightfully to the **triangular junction (P1)** below Ágios Sóstis. From there it is only another 20 quick minutes up to the "meeting place" in
1.40 **Ágios Andréas.** Complete with bus stop!

► Pasta fans will naturally want to try *matsata,* the local form of tagliatelle which is eaten both as a side-dish and as a main course.

Ios

The mountainous island has always attracted young rucksack tourists. This is understandable when one considers the picturesque Chóra with its narrow alleys, although these can be loud at night, and wide sandy beaches. Since the scarcity of water only permits a limited degree of agriculture, tourism provides a very welcome source of revenue. Despite the still prevalent sun-&-surf image of this "hippy" island, it is now also visited by families. A few old paths have been marked, and partly cleared as well, for hikers.
Hiking maps: Terrain # 315
Taxis: +30- 69777 60570, - 69770 31708

31 The conspiratorial monastery

Below Mount Elias are old mule tracks which ought to be brought back to life. Marked "3" and "1", they lead in 4½ hours to a green valley with a former monastery with spring and to sensational finds from the Bronze Age.
■ ***10 km, difference in altitude 330m, easy to moderate***

AWT From **Mill Square** at the upper edge of **Chóra** you walk
0.00 uphill, with the five upper mills soon on your left and the car park on the right. Continue up the concrete road until
0.05 you are led away from it to the right by the **steps** leading up to the Theatre O.T. The open-air theatre stays on your right, but pass it by. To the left of the chapel standing on

the wayside you discover a rocky path which winds its way through the rocks on the right of the next chapel. When the money still flowed from Brussels, a rather pompous and to this day empty museum was built here for the artist Gaitis. The monopáti forks after the third
0.10 **chapel** from 1894 ([1] p. 119)
Proceed up left, where you are immediately rewarded with a magnificent view. You see the unmistakable Santoríni, Chóra [1] and beyond it Síkinos. From the nice path [2] you later catch sight of the antennae of the Prophet Elías in the line of movement. Following a saddle you
0.25 come to a **hollow**, in the right-hand part of which are the remains of some houses. At the large triangular junction (**P1:** N36°43.711'/E25°17.738', 215m) you go up to the
!! right and *after 50m left* at a fork (the way to the summit straight ahead is overgrown).
At a dilapidated hut the distance between the walls be-
!! comes wider – keep walking halfway right, before taking
0.35 an *indistinct turn-off left* to a **saddle** with a dilapidated hut (**P2:** N36°43.881'/E25°17.910', 350m). From here you see wind rotors and soon afterwards the Prokópios monastery too, our first destination.
0.40 From the saddle the trail goes slightly downhill, a **chapel** stays down to the left. 11 minutes later you must not miss
0.50 the unclear **fork to the left.** It comes *ten metres before a*
!! *transversal gulley.* (**P3:** N36°44.069'/E 25°18.412', 330 m). In the valley you see a ruined chapel and the small monastery [3].

Short cut: Parts of the trail described below are unclear and overgrown, yet passable. One could turn back here.

At a sharp corner a goat track runs left downhill, to the left of a wall. To the right of the ruin of the chapel runs a monopáti. Regrettably this is so overgrown that one has to keep to the right of it like the goats until, after a few
1.10 prickly pears, you come to an empty **house.**
From there a somewhat tangly mule track runs downhill, but turns off to the left before the valley and joins the transversal path "2" going left to Chóra. Going right
1.20 brings you to the enclosure of the former **Ágios Prokópios Monastery** (**P4:** N36°44,379'/E25°18,367'). Today it is private property with terraced, charming gardens. The spring on the right offers good water.

In 1821 important personalities and captains assembled secretly in the isolated monastery in order to organise the uprising against the Ottomans.

The marked trail behind the monastery is so overgrown as to be impassable. But before the stream are two unlocked gates. Through these you cross the garden terraces down to the roadway and go left. Should the following driveway gate be closed, you have to go round it below on the right
1.35 and proceed down along the pretty lane to the **road.**
Now climb up right, past the Triáda chapel and a construction material store (left). After the hilltop, in a right-hand bend, you turn left on to a roadway (**P5:** N36° 44.071'/E25°18.409'). At the fork further down, below the hamlet **Elliniká**, our route runs to the right, through farming country.
Having passed a chapel (left), the dirt track swings to the left. Until recently there was a mule track here.
2.00 After the **Vasili chapel** (down right) the rest of the won-
★ derful mule track starts left, hewn into the terrain 4

(**P6:** N36°44,347'/E25°17,043'). Again you see Chóra with its 12 windmills. In front of it lie the fertile valley and the terraced hill of Skárkos. In the valley the path goes over a
2.10 **bridge**, then, lined by walls, up through olive groves and down to the ticket office for the excavation site in
2.20 **Skárkos.**

The excavations here revealed the oldest settlement of early Bronze Age Cycladic culture. The finds date back to 2,800 BC and are on display at Chóra Archaeological Museum. This site, which was abandoned 2,300 BC, once had two-storey houses, squares and streets.

Alternative: In continuation of the path leading here a kalderími runs straight on and up to **Chóra** in 15 minutes.

2.20 Otherwise you follow the seaward approach, which brings you past three giant eucalyptus trees to the sports field (right). Then you go right on the road, leave it to the
2.35 left after 100m and reach the **sea** via a dirt track.

Museum of Cycladic Art in Athens

Starting from Syntagma Square, it is a five-minute walk along Vasilissis Sofias Avenue to the *Museum of Cycladic & Ancient Greek Art* in Neofitou Douka St. 4.

This private museum has the most comprehensive collection of Cycladic idols on an area of 2,000 m^2.

On display here are about 350 exhibits from what is the oldest civilization in Europe as well as finds from the Neolithic and Hellenistic Ages. A visit to this museum is the perfect way to round off a trip to the Cyclades.

Open from 10 am to 4 pm, Saturdays until 3 pm, *closed Tuesdays and Sundays.*

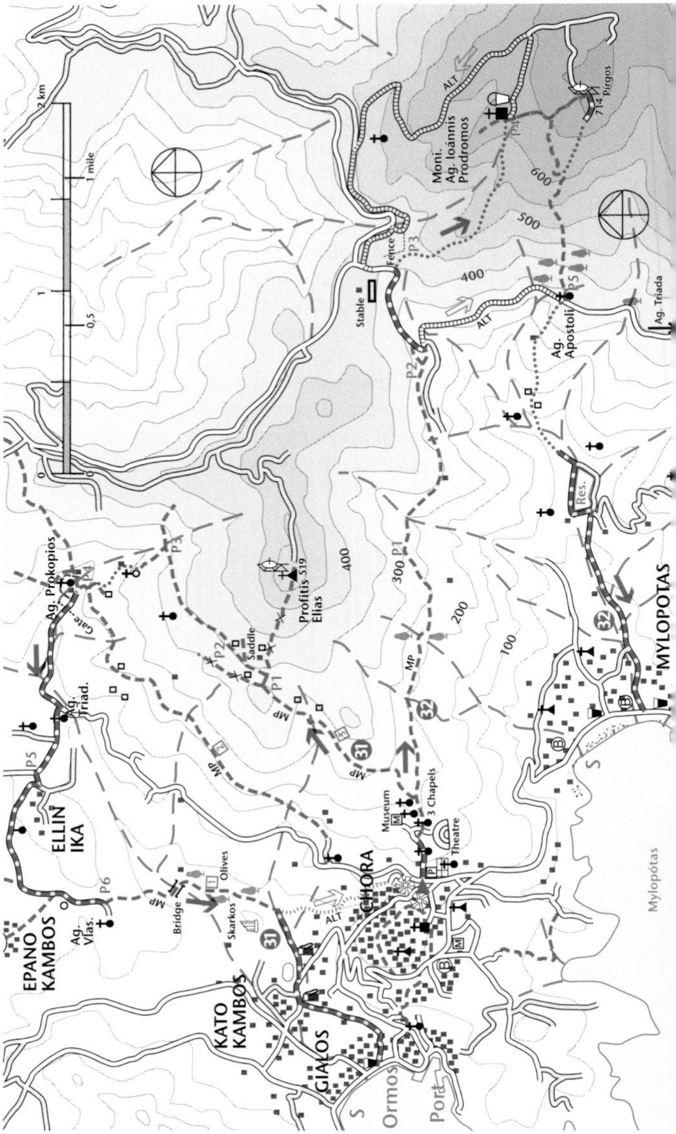
EPANO KAMBOS
KATO KAMBOS
GIALOS
Ormos
Port
CHORA
ELLINIKA
MYLOPOTAS
Mylopótas
Ag. Vlas.
Bridge
Skarkos
Olives
ALT
Museum
3 Chapels
Theatre
Ag. Triad.
Ag. Prokopios
Gate
Saddle
Profitis Elias
519
Stable
Fence
Ag. Apostoli
Ag. Triada
Res.
Moni.
Ag. Ioánnis
Prodromos
714
Pirgos
Ag. Triada
0
0,5
1
1 mile
2 km

㉜ On Pírgos

Ascending Pírgos, the highest point on Ios, takes 7 to 8 hours. For the way back there are two options. Either way, we have an enjoyable break on the terrace of the monastery of Agios Ioánnis with its superb views of the neighbouring islands. A shortened tour without summit ascent is also possible.
The pathless last stretch above Mylopótas is prickly!
■ 11 km, difference in altitude 580 or 714m, moderate or difficult

▷ *Map see left*

AWT From the barrier on the right of the five upper **windmills**
0.00 **of Chóra** (135m) we go up the concrete road, very soon
realising why the mills were built on this particular site,
and then follow the signs to the "Theatre O.E.". Some
0.05 **steps** soon lead straight uphill from the concrete road to
the first chapel (right). Behind it stands the new open-air
theatre.
Wonderful steps marked "3" lead past an empty picture
0.10 gallery and then, *after* the **third chapel** from 1894 [1], the
path forks. Heading left is ㉛. We walk straight on, soon
ending up completely alone on our attractive path [2]. A
thick water pipe is our sole companion for about 40 minutes. Ahead of us lies our goal, Mt. Pírgos with its antenna. Down in Mylopótas the bathing day slowly begins.
0.20 The path winds its way down to a **hollow** and, since parts
of it are overgrown, it is better to walk above it.
We continue over wide slabs of rock down to a cleft dot-

ted with oleander bushes which is green even in summer.
0.40 A couple of rocks form a wide **passage** (**P1:** N36°43.420′/E25°18.407′, 300m) across a further hollow. Later, after
1.00 opening a **gate** on the left, we behold the island's latest engineering achievement – the oversized road to Manganári. Already 100m before (**P2:** N36°43.362′/E25°19.149′, 335m) you leave the monopáti to the right in order to get
1.15 to the **road.**

> ***Short cut:*** If you go 900m *to the right* on the ascending road, you find the flat-roofed Apostle chapel on the left (AWT 2.55). From here you can descend to Mylopótas without a path.

Follow this road for eight minutes up *left.* Nature is already doing its best to create the normal road width. It is a relief to leave the asphalt again to the right before the left-hand bend and the steep embankment.

To the left of the green rift valley you come across faint tracks. At first you climb to the left of the rift up to the corner of a fence (**P3:** N36°43.410′/E25°19.574′, 425m). The continuation of the path is sometimes hard to locate, the wind turbine provides some guidance. Another 291 metres to climb! Approaching the saddle, down below you see a roadway, beehives and a green cleft. Parallel to the cleft several paths lead up the hill. Soon you see the monastery ③ up on the left. Do not cross the stream-bed too soon! Rampant heather covers every inch of the way,
1.45 but somehow we make it to the **Monastery of Ágios Ioánnis** (**P4:** N36°43.126′/E25°20.055′).

> *Not a bad place! A temple is said to have stood here in antiquity – quite understandable with this view!*
> *Stone benches and tables dominate the monastery grounds, the little locked chapel rather fading into the background. During the Panigíria, the parish festival on 20th June, eating and dancing seem to be the most important preoccupations. Our two panoramic terrace tables have been reserved for 35 people. Just hope they won't all come today!*

Two different routes present themselves for the way back. The descent to the beach of Mylopótas is arduous. Anyone looking for an easy way home should take the roadway at the rear of the monastery down to the road and then the already familiar path.

The more adventuresome climb up from the monastery
2.00 to the summit of **Mt. Pírgos** (714m) without a path. Here

you have a really superb view over to Santoríni, but are otherwise surrounded by rugged countryside and the hum of technology. From the viewing platform you bear right in the direction of Mt. Elias, gradually descending the slope until, half way between you and the big water reservoir, you spot the white Apostle chapel 4 directly on the road (the road cannot be seen on the photograph). This chapel is our destination.

The last 200m are somewhat strenuous, as the terrain is overgrown. On the right you can observe how the road engineers have tormented nature, which is now taking revenge on the poor hiker.

3.00 Below the flat-roofed **Apostle chapel** (**P:** N36°42.907'/ E25°19.355') you cross the road and, *dropping slightly,* head west towards the open sea and a few ruins, whose interiors give us an idea of their inhabitants' meager existence – hardly surprising that the younger generation has emigrated. We now climb up hill and down dale, keeping to the right towards Mt. Elias, as far as the mountain ridge. Everything is overgrown – and we search for a way down to the dilapidated houses and the olive trees on a hill above the site where the valleys converge. Once there, we wind our way down over crumbling terraces and head across a streamlet. Below a house we make for Mylopótas
3.35 **dam** and on to the **sea.** Into the water for a swim, on the
3.55 double now! The shuttle bus to Chóra runs until late evening.

33 A solitary strand

This circular trek of 4½ hours leads to a small, secluded sandy beach. The outward leg of the route leads through two cleft valleys without a trail, making orientation a little difficult, and along rocky slopes. We use old mule tracks for the return leg. There are no tavernas or cisterns en route. Long trousers are recommended.
■ 6 km, difference in altitude 110m, moderate to difficult

AWT In **Mylopótas** you alight at the bus stop at the end of the
0.00 bay. To the left of the **hotel** "Drakos" you go up the steps
0.10 and leave them to the left at room no. 9. Behind the
clothes lines you turn up right to a *black water tank*. 10m
beyond it a well-beaten track leads left up through rocky
terrain. After 80m a wall (right) accompanies the path
0.15 which, after a terrace, brings you through a **saddle** (**P1:**
N36°42.353′/E25°17.712′, 80m). On the slope on the left
is a ruin with tree, from where you will later return.
From the saddle tracks run straight on down through a
0.25 hollow and back up to an aloni, a **threshing floor** (**P2:**
36°42.225′/E25°17.716′). Now you keep halfway left,
without a path, down between magnificent boulders into
0.30 the **rift.** On the far side of the dry-bed, about 80m from
the water (**P3:** N36°42.055′/E25°17.905′) you proceed up
0.35 a narrow path to faint **paths.**
Follow these 50m to the left and then zig-zag your way
without a path up to a plateau, partly covered with white
marble (**P4:** N36°41.998′/E25°17.910′). It lies below the

peak. If you go around the mountain ridge on goat tracks, you have a better view of the goal: a sandy bay and a house 3.

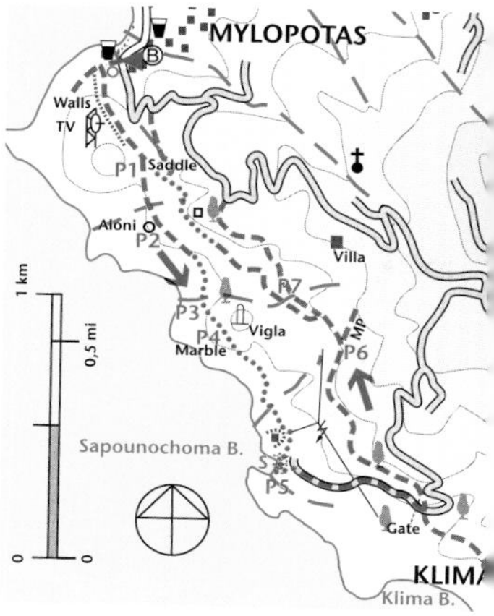

We have to scramble down over the bizarre, rocky coast; later on, we follow the remains of a path in the rift below. Going left around the tall garden wall of the house, you
0.55 reach the sandy bay of **Sa-**
★ **pounochoma.** The holiday house is mostly deserted (**P5:** N36°41.643′/ E25°18.092′). Now for a rest!

The way back begins on the gently ascending approach roadway heading inland. Im-
1.10 mediately left after the **gate** you find the ascending old path and turn on to this. (On the right is a path leading in 10 minutes to Klíma with holiday houses.) From the path (B4) we once again enjoy the view down to "our" bay and over towards Síkinos. Vertical stone slabs direct us like crash-barriers through the maze of rocks. After spotting a bunker-like villa up on the right, you must watch out carefully (**P6:** N36°41.987′/E25°18.248′, 120m): Do not
!! continue on the same level, but walk *down left* and
1.30 through a **defile!**

After that the now rather indistinct path leads half-left through rocks, through a rift with watercourse (P7: N36°42.060′/E25°18.084′) and back uphill again. About 150m below the "military" villa the path more or less follows the contour lines and leads, with a sea view, to the
1.45 **ruins** of the house with the tall tree.

Immediately next to that you cross a little wall and proceed horizontally below the sea of rock on flat slabs of rock to the left through a hollow to the saddle (**P1**), which you know from the way up. Below lies Mylopótas bay dotted with parasols, visible above is Chóra.
2.10 The already familiar trail runs down to the **hotel "Drakos".** You arrive there somewhat exhausted – the best thing would be to conjure up the key to room no. 9. But a drink on the hotel terrace is not a bad idea either!

Kímolos

Inhabited by just 600 people, this volcanic island still offers the hiker authentic island life, many intact mule tracks through green valleys and extensive terraces for the cultivation of cereals. Kímolos possesses sufficient water supplies and agriculture is commonly practised. Tourist facilities are the exception rather than the rule. While there is now enough accommodation.

Hiking maps: Anavasi #10.45 Terrain # 306
Road Tourist 1:20000 **Taxi:** +30 6945464093

34 Fields and terraces

This almost 3-hour circular tour affords an impression of the beautiful, cultivated landscape. The partly pathless ascent up to Kiriakí chapel is rather strenuous. Sufficient water rations and long trousers are advisable.
■ 6 km, difference in altitude 220m, moderate

WT At the **post office** (next to the telephone antenna) in the
.00 main street you go downhill, across the bridge, up the concrete path and then left. After the pension "Meltemi" (left) you take the basalt path going up right through ter-
.10 raced cornfields and after a big fork come to a **cistern** on the right (**P1:** N36°47.579'/E24°34.028', 100m).

From there you walk along a wonderful mule track down into the valley, right up the slope on the other side and then horizontally to the left along the edge of the hill. Af-

ter that you find yourself in a
gully, from where you go up *right*
after 40m. *Before* reaching a
0.20 **small wire door** (**P2:** N36°
47.700′/E24°33.738′) you climb
left up a steep monopáti, to-
wards the goal. Proceed straight
ahead at the right turn-off, then
0.25 right at the following **T-junction**
(**P3:** N36°47.756′/E24° 33.644′,
150m). Shortly afterwards the
stone walls spread out between
slabs of rock. Leave the inclined
and walled slab of rock on the
right and walk to wine and
0.35 **grain terraces** in a sloping valley. On the left an over-
grown path leads uphill, but it is easier to ascend on the
terraces and, half way up, open the fence on the far right
(**P4:** N36°47.824′/E24°33.582′). Up in the flatter part you
again see the flat-roofed chapel on the ridge over to the
right. Keeping to the right beneath the rock face, you
0.40 come without a path between bushes to the small **Kiriakí
chapel** (**P5:** N36°47.890′/ E24°33.620′). It is furnished in
peasant style. The amusing triptych depicts the transfor-
mation of the bearded Nicholas into Saint Lucia.
After the well-earned rest we continue up the hill which is
about 120m from the chapel in the direction of Poliégos.
Before that a rather overgrown monopáti winds its way
0.55 down to the **valley floor** (**P6:** N36°47'896′/E24°33.817′,
115m) and, diagonally vis-à-vis, uphill again to the wide
1.00 **gravel track.**
Climbing gradually, go left along the wide track as far as
1.10 the **grotto-like water basin in the rock** (left). The blue
notice warns people not to drink the water.
Opposite the water basin a monopáti branches off the
main track and drops down through a hollow covered
with olive tree terraces. With magnificent views of Chóra
(see previous page) and Poliégos you descend, turn right
1.20 at the **fork** in front of the fields and return along a path in
1.30 a deep cutting or in the stream-bed to **Chóra.**

35 The mushroom

Wandering on perfectly enchanting paths in 6 hours through the middle of the island we pass a natural monument, the "skiádi". From there on the trail is rather hard to find for about 10 minutes. As a reward, though, a magnificent sandy beach awaits us, where we can recover before strolling back across the fields to Chóra.
■ 17 km, difference in altitude 280m, moderate to difficult

AWT The OTE **antenna** in the centre of the village is not diffi-
0.00 cult to find. Setting off from here, leave the village by going north along the main alley and, at a fork, straight
0.03 ahead as far as the **bus stop** beside a power transformer at
0.05 the fork. Now turn left into the **dry stream-bed**, right after the bridge and alongside the stream-bed. Before the next bridge take the concrete path going up to the left. A few years ago this was still a paved kalderími. Proceeding outside the village, walk up a low-lying track between the fields, past two left turn-offs, and on uphill the whole time in the direction of the radar reflector standing over to the right on the summit and serving as a point of reference. Between two houses on either side the path to Kyri-
0.10 akí chapel 34 **turns off** to the left.
0.20 Having passed a **watering-place** hewn out of the rock (left), you come to Anargíri chapel, whose strange new door is locked. Ignore the right turn-off down to Vasilius
0.30 chapel and the **left turn-off** up to the Exo church. Rounding a right-hand bend, you stand above a wide valley, at

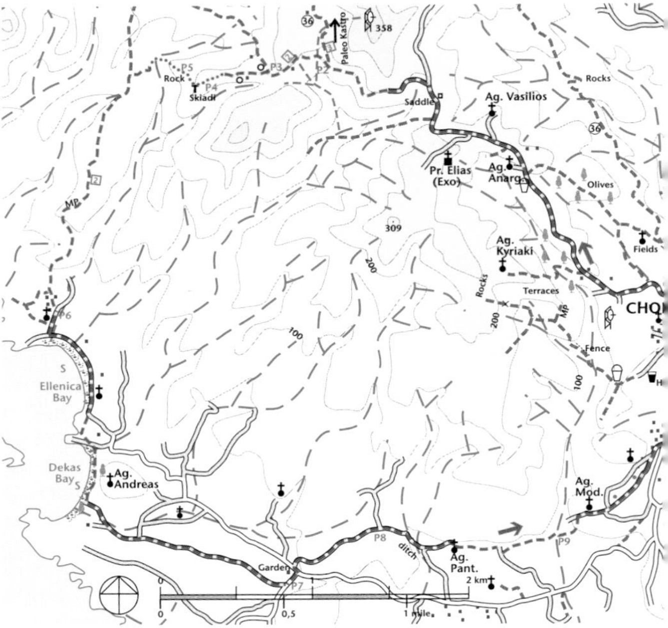

the end of which lies the lading port for bentonite – a clayey volcanic rock which is locally quarried, much less obtrusively than on Mílos.

You traverse a saddle, on the right-hand side of which is a

0.40 ruin, and come to the **fork** above which is written "Skiadi" (**P1:** N36°48.525′/E24°33.295′, 230m). A roadway runs a further 300m left, doubtless for the hikers from "Miloterranian Geowalks", who can comfortably park their cars here. The thereby shortened path is marked "2" and "3".

On the left lies a splendid valley, criss-crossed by a

★ monopáti. It is possible to see the white Sarakíniko coast of Mílos ①. This breathtaking sight makes amends for the radar reflector up on the right.

0.50 Later the **right turn-off** (**P2:** N 36°48.593′/ E 24°32.905′, 280m) leads up to the island's old Byzantine capital Palíokástro ㊱.

Turn right in front of a house and down left at the fork

above the round threshing area (**P3:** N36°48.565′/E24° 32.662′). Then head for this curious mushroom-shaped stone which has been visible for some time now. At a house with small threshing area the beautiful, wall-lined
1.05 path ends. Cross a flat rock to reach the **skiádi**, the mushroom ② (**P4:** N36°48.534′/E24°32.372′). A flat lump of rock lying on soft sandstone whose lower part has been sanded down by the wind in the course of time. This transient natural monument affords us shade for a brief respite.

! For concentration is required from here on! *Go right* at a 90° angle to the track used up to now, down across white ledges of sandstone, past some cairns and towards a wide rock ③. To the right of it (**P5:** 36°48.573′/E24°32.324′)
! watch out for *indistinct* tracks, finally dropping down into the hollow at a wall. You are welcome to add more cairns!

Shortly before you reach the dry stream-bed the path be-
.15 comes more distinct again, leading left through the **ditch** and up to the broad monopáti which approaches from the right. It runs left to the sea, in the direction of Mílos, so we do not hesitate to join it. It is all plain sailing now. Just having to trample a few thorny companions underfoot. The wonderful panorama path ④ leads into a stream-bed (**P6:** N36°47.851′/E24°31.824′) and brings you
.55 to **Ellinikå Bay.** Gravel – if you prefer something softer, amble left along the shore, looking out at the many rocks which seem to dance in the sea like elves.

The rocky headland and the island beyond used to be connected. This is the site of the ancient town of Límni, which was abandoned during the Byzantine era.

2.10 Behind the fantastically shaped rocky headland **Déka**
Bay offers the finest sand and tamarisks. Thanks to the
shallow water, bathing temperatures are already inviting
in spring. And we have certainly earned a dip. If you order
a taxi in advance, you can extend the pleasure for even
longer.
Sooner or later the more sporty among us have to get go-
2.15 ing and start walking along a dirt track running **inland**
through the coastal plain. At the fork go right through
2.35 gardens and fields, reaching the **road** (**P7:** N36°46.848'/
E24°32.727') on level ground.
Proceed left along the road for only 80m – but without
missing the rock garden with prickly pears and wine.
Where the road forks, you turn left for 20m until you
2.40 reach a **dirt track** on the right which, bordered by walls,
runs along the coastline. The shipowner family Ventouri
occasionally resides on the little island over to the right.
2.45 Later the track **forks** – you go right along a ditch (**P8:**
N36°47.013'/E24°33.796') and back up again. Disregard
the following right turn-off, instead taking a path starting
2.50 at the sharp-edged **Panteleimon chapel** (right).
After a ditch (**P9:** N36°47.042'/E24°33.796') you walk up-
hill for quite a while, at the end on a dirt track, until com-
3.10 ing to the **Modestos chapel** (left) beside a water pond.
From there you continue straight ahead and past another
pond (left).
Gradually the houses rise up out of the hollow. After pass-
ing through a "suburb", you cross a bridge and return to
3.25 **Chóra**.

▶ **Accommodation:**	Villa María (Chóra)	22870 513 92
	Meltémi (Chóra)	22870 513 60
	Prezianis	22870 512 85
	Sardi (Aliki Beach)	22870 514 58
	Aliki	22870 513 40

㊱ The abandoned Paliókastro

This trek to the uninhabited north mostly follows paths and lasts, with the "full programme", more than 8 hours. Agióklima bay could be omitted, however. The treeless route has few waterholes, but none which have drinking water quality. The "nature" experience is in the foreground, nothing of the former island capital Paliókastro remains to be seen.
■ 20 km, difference in altitude 320m, difficult

AWT Follow the description for ㉟ as far as AWT 0.50. At the
0.50 **turn-off** to the right (**P2:** N36°48.593'/E24°32.905', 280m) are a few paved sections leading up to a small
1.00 house [1]. From the **saddle** you overlook the broad expanse of sea without islands. The path becomes narrower and heads towards the castle hill, on the left side of which the old city used to lie [2]. Later the path winds its way
1.15 down across a smooth **rocky expanse** (**P3:** N36°49.083'/ E24° 32.827', 305m) and comes to another saddle with ruined houses. From there it ascends again and traverses a gap in the rock, before reaching a pool in the rock (right) (**P4:** N36°49,246'/E24°32,779'). At the next slight descent you can try to make out remains of the old city up to the right.

*The **Paliókastro** stood on the right-hand side of the hill and was the capital of the island until the arrival of the Venetians in the 16th century. However a lay visitor cannot discern any traces of settlements.*

1.25 On the left-hand side of the path is a large **threshing floor** (**P5:** N36°49.386'/E24°32.767'). The arduous de-

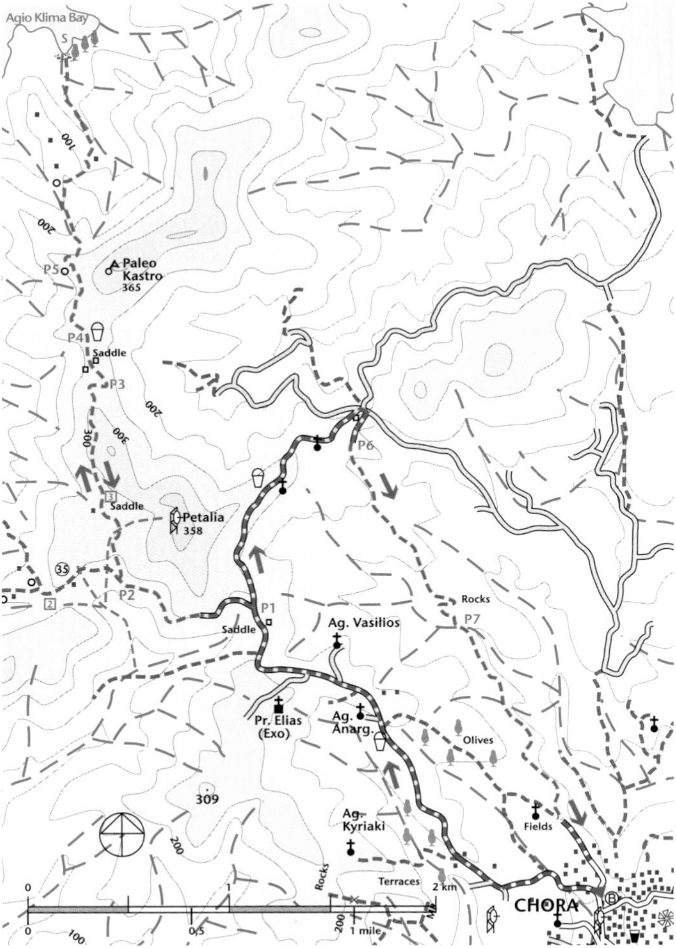

scent to the sea begins here, albeit with a fabulous view 3. Initially the trail is easy to identify as it heads for a weirdly shaped rock face, before dropping further down with two shed down to the right. Then the track ends and it is necessary to force your way down through scrub to the
2.00 sandy beach of **Agióklima.**

2.40 The ascent back up to the **col** with the threshing floor calls for quite a bit of stamina. But thereafter the going gets easier, because flatter. Again passing the waterhole
2.50 (left) to reach the **saddle with the ruins,** you come to the
3.10 **turn-off** from the main path (**P2**) and walk left to the
3.25 **fork** from the roadway (**P1**). Those who wish to take a short cut go right there to the already familiar way down to the **Chóra** (AWT: 4.00).

3.25 Those still full of energy proceed left up the roadway on
3.35 the left at this **fork,** past another waterhole (left) and two
3.45 chapels (right) and down to a large **crossing.** Here you turn sharp right, rambling past a house ruin (right) and through an artificial gap. Beyond this the roadway drops left and becomes a monopáti (**P6:** N36°48.885'/E24° 33.616', 195 m). Perhaps somewhat overgrown in spring,
4.00 this later leads through **rocks** and zig-zags down into a
4.05 **stream-bed** (**P7:** N36°48.459'/E24°33.945', 110m). After an ascent it runs flat and straight as an arrow, without any
4.30 forks, to the village [4]. You reach the **Chóra** roughly where you started this morning.

Kíthnos

The relatively flat, rather barren island is on account of its hot springs a favourite destination of Greek health spa visitors. The island's proximity to Athens can lead to problems in finding accommodation at the weekends. But, apart from yachtsmen, international tourism passes Kíthnos by, which is precisely what makes this tranquil island so attractive. Wonderful old footpaths still exist. Shady trees are however an absolute rarity. A regular bus service operates from mid-June until mid-September.
Hiking maps: Anavasi # 10.44 Terrain # 302
Taxi: +30 – 6944-271609 / 6944-276656 / 6944-743791

37 1537

In the fateful year 1537 almost all the Cycladic islands were occupied by the Turks. This 4-hour trek along old tracks starts at the spa resort of Loutrá and follows the traces of the Turkish conquerors right up to the ruin of the Venetian fortress Kastro Oriás (also Paléo Kástro). Unlike the warriors of those days we do not have to carry heavy gear with us, just food and water rations, for wholly trustworthy cisterns are in short supply. On the way back we permit ourselves a small beach.
■ 10 km, difference in altitude 260m, moderate

1

2

AWT **Loutrá thermal bath** *has sulphurous and iron-rich springs of up to 52° which have been in use since Antiquity. Even king Otto I and his spouse Amalie sought relief here. Today the harbour attracts many sailors.*

0.00 On the right of the old **Healing Water Source**, which is assembled out of grey blocks of marble, you ascend the wide stairway. After a short flat part further steps lead up to a well-beaten track. This merges into a roadway after
0.10 two minutes. Having reached a **little road** at the end of the valley, go 50m left to the main road and right there.
0.15 After about 150m 1 the trained eye finds the old **footpath** running down to the left opposite a ruin (**P1:** N37°24.690'/E24°26.547'). The monopáti marked "1" drops gently down into the valley, where you soon come
0.20 across reeds and a **well** by the wayside. 100m further on you go left at the fork beside an olive grove and later, after the fig tree above the deeply carved in path (where a deep
0.30 well lies concealed), you go left up the **transversal monopáti** (**P2:** N37°27.214'/E24°25.208', 110m).
0.40 Where it **joins** a dirt track (**P3:** N37°27.416'/E24°25.066'), we go left. The track, which can now be negotiated by robust vehicles, leads to a wide fork at the top near the
0.45 chapel of **Agios Fílippos** (right) (**P4:** N37°27.598'/E24° 24.956', 220m). Here we go left to the goat-sheds, where we soon pick out our destination for the day, the ruins of the fortress 2. After a wide gate we keep halfway left, following the white markings, pass a lattice door and find the path on the left side of the hill in the foreground. This
1.00 leads to the entrance of the **fortress.**

Those in search of something more dramatic walk without a path to the left of a wall, passing through a

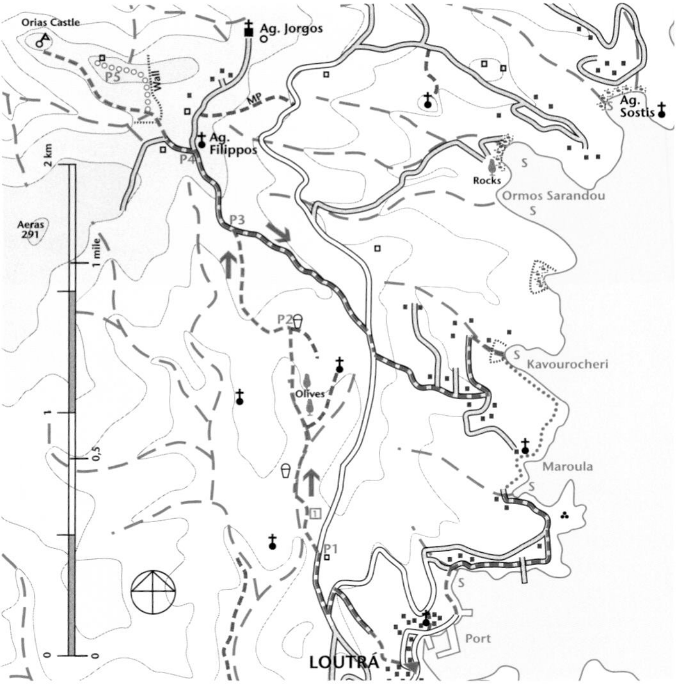

gateway, and on up to the **rocky hill** beyond (**P5:** N37°27.748'/E24°24.763'). Here you have a magnificent view of the enormous lump of rock upon which stood the Venetian fortress **Kástro Oriás** 2. In the background lies the island of Kéa.

At this very spot where the Ottoman warriors lay in wait that night in the year 1537. The Venetians had dug a moat in front of the fortified town. It did not help against the ruse of war employed by the Turkish admiral Chaireddin Barbarossa: an expectant mother knocked on the gates and asked to be let in. As the gates opened, the sultan's warriors stormed the fortress. Only three of more than 400 inhabitants who had sought refuge there survived the massacre alive.

Below the fortress on the left you pass through the gate decorated with crosses and easily find the path up to the

1.05 **Church of the Mother of God** (Kíra Eleoúsa) which was later built among the ruins. You will find a water tank here. Further down, between the destroyed houses, stands the vaulted Trinity church.
The way back leads along the side of the foothill and to
1.25 the **Fílippos chapel** again. On the already familiar dirt track you go down right and, past where the monopáti
1.35 turns off to the right, to the **road.** Here you go 70m right and then left down the roadway to the sea 3. At a T-junction near holiday houses you turn left and come, further
1.50 down at an enclosed property, to **Kavourochéri beach.**
Below a wall goat paths 4 lead on along the shoreline. Af-
2.00 ter a holiday house with **chapel** on the right, you come to a driveway at the next bay. You now traverse a peninsula on which were found the oldest traces of settlements in the Aegean from the 7th century B.C. After a bathing bay you pass beneath the old ore loading installations which have been rusting away for 60 years. We certainly haven't started to rust today, so proudly take a seat beneath a
2.15 tamarisk in **Loutrá** and let the waiter do the running for a change.

38 Old rivals

The only two villages in the interior of the island are Kíthnos and Driópis, also known as Chóra and Chórico (village). Each has always claimed to be the more beautiful place. Today we are going to decide for ourselves.
Both villages used to be connected by a flagstone path, which had to make way for motorized traffic. However this road is not the only connection. The 2½- hour trail described here also leads to the chóra, but the undergrowth is knee-high in three places – a clear case for long trousers.
■ 8 km, difference in altitude 70m, easy to moderate

AWT **Driópis** is can only be reached by taxi in low season. The village, whose appearance is almost Spanish (see p. 134), is hardly geared to tourism. Yet the beauty of the settlement and its surrounding topography is at least equal to that of the chóra.

0.00 From the **forecourt of the twin-towered church** you walk downhill for about 30m and go straight down the steps beside the bakery (left). After 37 steps, above the valley, descend more steps left to a concrete path. Wander slowly down it, between the walls, to the green and shady valley bottom.

0.05 **Whitewashed steps (P1:** N37°23.097'/E24°25.715') 1 lead up to the right and then, after 10m, on to the left at the fork. You climb on the right above the valley, after a bend you see a chapel with mini-tambour in a side valley and to the left of it our onward track in a saddle. Having

1

2

traversed the floor of the side valley - which may be overgrown in spring – we stroll alongside gardens and a cis-
0.15 tern (right) to a **turn-off** below a chapel (**P2:** N37°23.361'/ E24° 25.619').

Here we go straight up the winding, rather overgrown monopáti as far as the saddle (200m) with a crossing of the ways, where we go straight ahead. After 50m we come to a
0.25 second **fork** (**P3:** N37° 23.562'/E24°25.721') above a ruined house, from where we can see our destination behind a flat mountain ridge – the strung-out chóra, flanked by wind rotors.

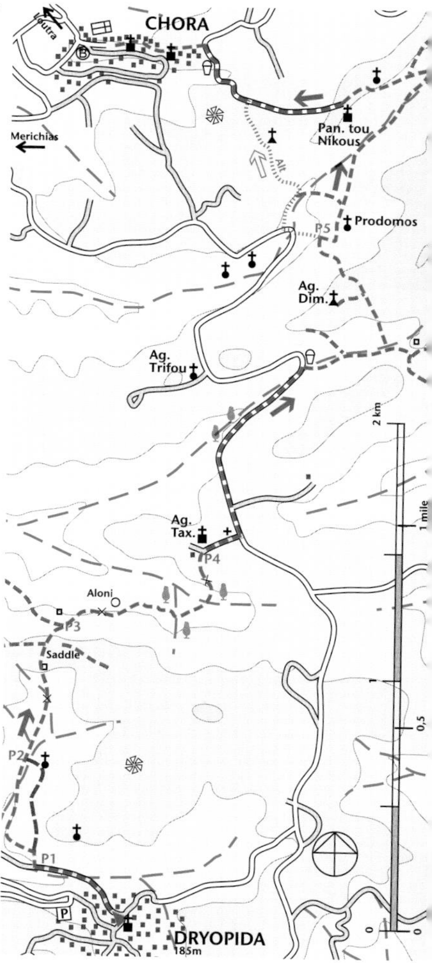

At this fork you go right along the mule track, following the contour lines. On the left-hand side of the counterslope you can make out two intermediate goals: a domed church and, to the left above it, on the next slope, another chapel. The path now descends into the valley and is also covered with knee-high spherical spurge for about 50m. Before
).40 the **hollow** you encounter thick oleander. From there you ascend through denser undergrowth (perhaps to the left of the path) and, after a farmhouse (left), find the very
).50 old, three-aisled **taxiarchis/archangel church** ②, which

3

4

was constructed with ancient columns and capitals and
decorated with frescoes (**P4:** N37°23.780′/E24°25.657′).
Along the driveway you come to the road – up until 15
years ago still a kalderími. The ten minutes left on asphalt
are soon over. Forking right before the stream-bed is a
path which, at the *second left turn-off,* leads to the route of
tour ㊴. Here you go left over the hill, on the left of which
stands the Dimitrios chapel. Below, above a dip, one
1.10 could go left at the **T-junction** (**P5:** N37°24.387′/E24°
26.308′, 170m) and follow ㊴ from AWT 3.35.
However if you prefer to amble further through the coun-
tryside [3], turn right here and proceed along the dip past a
chapel (right) until you can see the Nicholas chapel above
1.35 right ([1] next page) and a **path crosses.** Here you turn up
left and saunter, past the large Panagia tou Nikous
1.55 monastery (left), down a concrete track into the **Chóra.**
This village [4] is much more geared to tourism than
Driópis. The fabric-covered chairs of the inns are sup-
posed to engender international flair. Yet the normal cane
chairs in Driópis, though rickety, would be just as fitting.

39 A long day's hike …

… which can be split by arranging to be picked up by taxi in Ágios Stéphanos! The village also has inns in summer. The nearly 8-hour tour runs almost entirely on marked paths!
■ 15 km, difference in altitude 275m, difficult

WT In the Chóra you set off from the ΔΗΜΑΡΧΕΙΟ, or **town-**
.00 **hall.** While passing through the town, you first see a
square on the right, followed by the church Ágios Theoló-
gos (right). After strolling along an alley, take the second
one, which drops slightly to the left past a church roof
.05 (right). At the "dead" **well** at end of the alley go right,
through a dip. Take the transversal concrete track and af-
.15 ter 50m, up right at the fork to the church **Panagía tous**
Nikous.
Using the same path, you then continue downhill, first
on a left-hand turn-off and then, above the dip, past a
.25 *right-hand turn-off*. The path crosses this **dip** and runs up-
hill, past the Nicholas chapel 1 (**P1:** N37°24.692'/E24°
26.624', 280m). At the very top you come to a large trian-
.35 gular **fork** (**P2:** N 37°24.639'/E 24°26.935') at a threshing
floor.
Here you ramble on to the left, with Loutrá bay on your
.40 left. After crossing a **dirt track**, you keep going uphill.
.45 Further up you branch off to the **right** (**P3:** N37°24.767'/
E24°27.241', 275 m). Below a St. Mary's chapel the path 1
.50 leads into a green **valley.** From there the monopáti as-
cends again for seven minutes through an uninhabited
.00 region to a **level section**, before you lose height on wide

1.20 slabs of rock. Awaiting the hiker in the **valley** is a field o oleander bushes and a few rock pools. From there step lead, past a St. George's chapel, up to an "interchange (**P4:** N37°24.187′/E24°27.292′,135m). You will pass thi point again later.

First, though, you ascend left over a mountain ridge and at the end of the long trail, see the bay down below (B3) After a short detour you can pleasurably stretch out be
1.45 neath a tamarisk at **John's bay.**
2.05 You have to climb back up to **point P4.** Here a path run left for four minutes and is then blocked at an opening ir a wall. Beyond the blockage well-beaten ruts lead half-lef down to a passage through the wall.

From there you go right until, where the field wall ends (at a wire fence), you encounter an overgrown roadway, which circumvents the valley. Behind another fence you find a monopáti running down to **Stephan's bay** with two seasonal inns.

You head inland along the road as far
2.35 as a **right-hand turn-off** into the valley (**P5:** N37°23.972′/E24°27.286′).
2.45 Follow the **roadway** left and, *at the*
!! *first electricity pole,* right. Ten meters further on an indistinct, short roadway branches off to the right (**P6:** N37°23.996′/E24°27.189′).

In front of a gate made of metal rods a mule track sets off to the right, running round the farmhouse standing

higher up and then ascending to the left. Soon it reaches a
2.50 **chapel** and leads you, dropping again, above the valley
3.00 on the left. At a **fork** you descend left to the stream-bed of a side valley with oleander bushes (**P7:** N37°24.087'/ E24°26.824').

The first metres uphill after that are prickly. Overcome a blockage by bearing right, then climb steeply up to the right. The walls widen out, enabling you to make serpentine bends on rocky ledges. On the following horizontal
3.20 section a path **branches** off right to a chapel [4] (**P8:** N37° 24.145'/E24°26.541', 220m). But you proceed straight ahead.

!! The path winds its way into a dip where, after 40m, a *path leads you up to the right.* In the next dip, at a T-junction (**P9:** N 37°24.387'/E 24°26.308', 170 m), you go left to the
3.35 **road** and there right.

On the other side of the valley, after 50m, you reach a rather overgrown monopáti. Having taken you over a hill,
3.50 it brings you back into the **Chóra.** Proudly you amble through the alleyways and, later, try to keep your eyes open in the taxi.

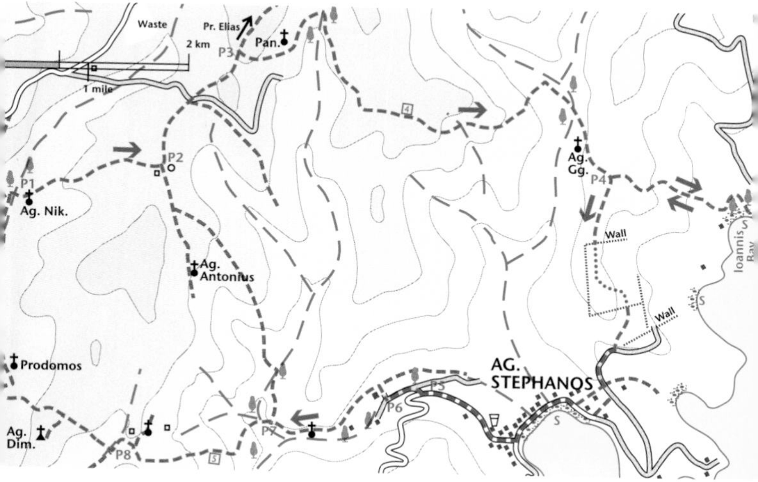

Mílos

The flat mining island lies on the south Aegean seismic arc (see page 10). It was built up gradually in layers formed by volcanoes. One of the volcanoes is still active today, albeit on a small scale. The Bay of Mílos is not a caldera, however, having been formed by displacement.
The natural beauty-spots of this rather barren island predominantly face the sea. The mining industry has led to massive intrusions into the natural landscape – that is why one almost only finds dirt roads in the eastern part of the island. More suitable for hiking is the lonely, western half below the Profítis Elías, only accessible by hire car. Mílos also makes a good starting point for walks on Kímolos.
Hiking maps: Anavasi # 10.45, Terrain # 306
Taxis: +30-22870-22119

40 Dream coast

This four to five-hour hike leads along the north coast without paths. The beaches only have tavernas in season and are partly deserted.
The second part of the trek mostly leads through wonderful rock formations.
■ 9 km, difference in altitude 70m, easy

Take the Pollónia bus to **Fylakopí** excavations.
Fylakopí was the first capital of the island and the centre of the obsidian trade with the whole Mediterranean region.

Excavations have unearthed four towns built on top of each other, dating from between 2300 and 1100 BC. The frescoes discovered have now been moved to the National Museum in Athens. On site it is still possible to make out a huge defence wall of cyclopean stonework and the ground plan of interlocking houses.

AWT The trek begins at the **car park** to the left of the fence at
0.00 the site. It is easy to find the rocky path between the road and the sea which leads you to a sandy bay between the
0.05 cliffs in five minutes. Having gone over a **bridge of rock,** then directly above the water, you arrive in the holiday
0.10 resort of **Papáfraga/Páchena.** Taking the asphalt path near the sea, you arrive, next to a guesthouse (left), at a
0.15 wide **sandy bay.** Nimble walkers can manage to reach the far end without getting wet. There
0.20 a **roadway (P1:** N36°45.148/E24° 29.660') leads to a sort of heath and then back down towards the rocky shore. Seagulls from the island of Glaronissiá vis-à-vis do low-flying exercises here in spring. At the end of the rugged, scree landscape is
0.30 the small **barrel-**

roofed church of Agios Konstantínos and a second chapel. Not until you get closer do you see the hidden small fishermen's houses and the harbour [1]. The rock in the sea ahead forms a double-spanned bridge. At the edge of the church wall starts a white path over solidified lava above a huge grotto, which is not recognizable as such
0.35 until later. After the large **sandy bay** follows another smaller bay. Now it is possible to walk right out along the spit, before carrying on over the flat rock directly at the water's edge. Having broken away and now been separated from the mainland by a five-metre stretch of water, a large rock is occupied by raucous seagulls in spring. We jump over long, narrow crevices in which the water bubbles. This unreal landscape [2] was created by the rock being compacted under repeated pressure and earthquakes. The remaining vegetation has been forced to the ground by the wind. The rock pools are large enough to take a re-
1.00 freshing bathe. The natural harbour of **Mytakas**, with strand and picturesque small houses, lies at the bend on the coastline (**P2:** N36°44.603'/E24°28.688').

Having gone round the harbour, we reach a wide sandy bay with tamarisks and hewn grottos. Above this begins
★ the wondrous world of the **Sarakíniko Coast.** [3]. First traverse a ditch near the sea. Walk round the bay which follows and, on the far side (**P3:** N36°44.502'/E24°28.328'), hug the shoreline for quite a long section.

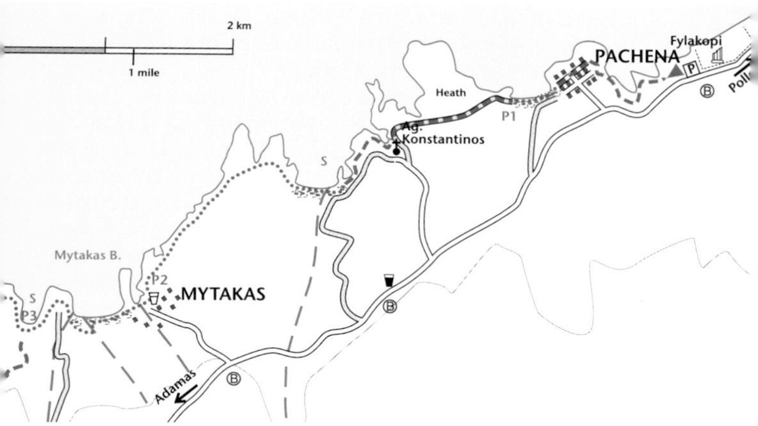

The coast consists of sandstone and limestone, eroded and polished into bizarre shapes by wind and water. It is undoubtedly one of the most beautiful coastlines in Europe ④. Flat rocks lie in the water; the steep cliffs rising up from the sea sometimes take on the appearance of a herd of elephants at a watering place. Wandering later above the cliffs, you feel as if you were among desert dunes and
1.30 then come past a **boat garage** and a shipwreck.
All of a sudden people are everywhere, tripping over each other to take pictures. For five minutes further up is a car park and a (seasonal) bus stop. Down below is a popular
1.40 **bathing cove.**

> ***Alternative:*** The sporty among us go round this cove and clamber over the chalk cliffs beyond. Keep halfway left up across the gravelly, barren region as far as a roadway, which leads you to the picturesque fishing village of **Mantrákia** with the recommendable taverna *Medusa* in 25 minutes.
> From there, however, you have another 25 minutes before reaching the bus station in Péra Triovássalos.

Pleasure-seekers remain on the Sarakíniko Coast for a while, enjoying the rounded formations. When our eyes are sated, we put our shoes back on, walk up to the main road in about twelve minutes, then turn right along it for 100m before heading to the left near the power pole and over the ridge without a path. The huge Bay of Mílos, Ormos Miloy, is visible below and we find paths and tracks
2.15 over some fairly unremarkable terrain down to **Adámas.**

41 The last volcano

In the south-east of the island is the large extinct volcano Tsigrádo, which forms an extensive round crater with tilled fields.
The 5-hour circular tour starting from Zerifíria takes you along dirt tracks and narrow trails to a sub-crater, where you can smell the bad breath from the bowels of the earth. Before that you pass through a landscape which is quite untypical of the islands. A certain surefootedness is necessary on the way down to the sea. In season a beach bar is open.
■ 10 km, difference in altitude 120m, moderate

Zefiría *was the island's main town until 1750, with 5000 inhabitants. Now it only has 200.*
Following an earthquake in Santoríni the earth emitted sulphurous vapours here which contaminated the air and the soil. When diseases broke out, the town was abandoned around 1750. The more than 400-year-old church Panagía Portianí, the island's former episcopal church, lay in ruins for a long time and was only rebuilt 100 years ago. It has been almost completely painted again.

AWT 0.00 From the church walk back to the **main road** and left along the road at the sign "Paliochóri", past the rather sophisticated restaurant *Petrino* (left). Already after 150m, though, you turn right on to a dirt track which is lined by extra-wide walls on the left. In the direction of sight and movement you see the mighty Profítis Elías; on the left tower the edges of the crater. It is only possible to discern the outlines of the cutaway entrance.

0.10 The trail approaches the **airport**, on the perimeter of which you turn left, then go round the corner and along the fence (right) for 120m. At the edge of the wall surrounding an olive grove (left) you turn off to the left (**P1:** N36°41.805'/E24°28.944'). In the direction of movement you see greenhouses. This region is called *Kámpos* and is the island's granary. The fertile volcanic soil is used to cultivate not just corn, but potatoes, tomatoes, grapes and vegetables. Straightforward, unspectacular farming country.

0.20 At a T-fork you go left to the **greenhouses** with a row of cypress trees. At the T-fork beyond them you turn left and

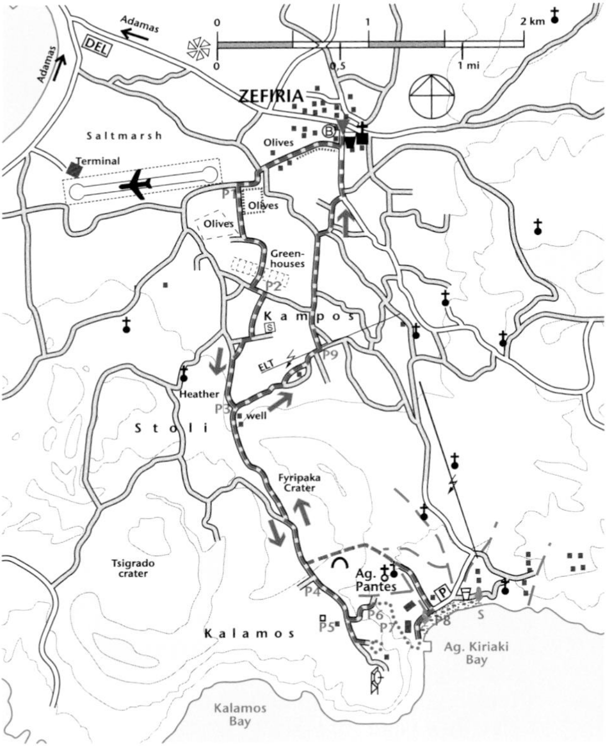

after 40m right again (**P2:** N36°41.408′/E24°29.051′), thus continuing in the same direction. You pass a strange building topped by a large concrete frame. It is one of several wells in the region. They were used up until 2000. Later you notice a solar plant on the left-hand side of the route.

Having passed the fields, you come to a heath with juniper trees. You turn right at the next T-fork and then left at the following triangular "traffic island" after 30m. Fields have been laid out at the very edge of the crater,
0.35 higher up is scrub. In this area, called ***Stóli,*** stands a pump room (**P3:** N36°40.988′/E24°28.926′). Go right here.

A narrow valley leads you into the **Fyriplaka crater.** It has a diameter of 1,700 meters and arose about 400,000 years

ago. Today it is covered with cornfields which form a
0.45 bizarre contrast with the dark green cedars [1]. At a **right-hand bend** (**P4:** N36°40.555′/E24°29.152, 75m) you march briskly straight on up until you come to the red-tinged rocky ledge overlooking the sea. The region is also called Kálamos.

Below to the left you see the coastal plain of Agios Kiriakí [2], with Folégandros in the background; up on the right stands an antenna. The dirt track forks at a fairly large
1.00 **building** (**P5:** N36°40.109′/E24°25.462′). We are drawn towards the red cliffs. First go left, but veer right into an area surrounded by rocks 80m before a barn. Everywhere the earth's crust emits hissing sulphurous vapours. Walk across the eerily beautiful spot in a clockwise direction, where you will even find a tunnel, and return to the large
1.15 **building.**

There tracks branch off to the right, which you follow
!! downhill. But in the *second bend to the left* (**P6:** N36°40,209′/E24°29,458′), after approx. three minutes, you go straight ahead and leave the dirt track. A path leads left between two prominent bushes in the direction of the coastal plain. Then you continue downhill on the boundary be-
1.20 tween field and scrub. After a **fence** you go through some rocks – then bear right. Markings help you down the not very steep descent, but a certain surefootedness helps. Later on the corn terraces keep right in the direction of the jetty.

1.40 At the **shore** you come, through a glorious muddle of usable and unusable objects, to a fine sandy beach with tamarisks and a pleasant beach cafe.

From cafe retrace your steps for 100m. Standing in the

middle of the beach is an empty, two-storey building. (To the left of it a signpost "Agios Pantes" points in the wrong direction.) A further 30m left/south of this we go up the steep roadway (**P8:** N36°40.241'/E24°29.842'). On your right you see narrow eroded ravines with almost vertical pumice stone walls.

Plodding sternly on up through the grey region, the
1.45 **Pántes chapel** (left) and the ruins of its predecessor chapel on the opposite side of the ravine provide a welcome diversion. From there you proceed through unusual, undulating layers of featherweight perlite as far as the
1.55 **edge of the crater.**

From up here you again see the large fields inside the crater. First to the left, then to the right of the fence you
2.05 make your way down to the already familiar **dirt track.**
2.20 Walk back along this to the **pump rooms of Stóli** (**P3:** see above) and then turn right at the fork. Now you roam over field and meadow, heading for the white domes of the church in Zefiría, which from a distance looks more like a mosque.
2.25 Go left at the fork, at the next **fork** beneath the power line likewise, and continue towards the village. Go
2.30 straight ahead briefly at the **junction** where a track joins from the right, then turn left at the turn-off (**P9:** N36°41.185'/E24°29.319'). The greenhouses lie far away to the left.

The hills surrounding the plain bear witness to the ubiquity of the local mining industry. Approaching the village
2.40 you turn off to the right at the **signpost** "Ag. Kiraki", then 80m afterwards left at the next one. Walk left along the
2.50 road into **Zefiría**, where you could give *Petrino's* cuisine a try.

42 A long history

A 4-hour trek from Adámas to the most important historic sites and places of cultural interest on the island. It is advisable to wear long trousers – not just because of the sacred places, but also to protect your legs! Large stretches lead without a path above the sea, offering a magnificent view of the bay. However it is possible to avoid the two difficult passages. Klíma has a place to stop at. In low season the catacombs are only open until 1 pm!

■ 7 km, difference in altitude 170 m, moderate to difficult

AWT 0.00 On the left beside the **tourist information** at the jetty in **Adámas** are public hot springs in caves such as were found all over the island in earlier times. They are open in the mornings. We follow the shore promenade to north to Lagáda bay. To the right of the Beach Hotel is the entrance to the 250m deep World War II shelters which were created for the German occupying troops and the civilian population.

Alternative: The route described here leads across open terrain without any markings, climbing gently without a path for 25 minutes. If you wish to avoid this, go round the hotel and, 400m further up, take the second left turn-off up away from the road. A dirt track leads in a left bend round the hill with the antenna to **P2** in 30 min. This variant has no sea views to offer, though.

The more interesting route leads directly along the edge

1

2

of the water and on over a hilltop to a more peaceful bay. Here we come across a graveyard and a monument from 1897. It was set up in memory of the Frenchmen who died of the plague here in the harbour, aboard the ships of the expedition corps during the Crimean War (1853–56). French influences were felt on Mílos from 1800. French soldiers also found their final resting-place here during the First World War.

The vast natural harbour, one of the largest in the Mediterranean, has always been of great strategic importance and was the cause of the repeated conquests of the island through the ages.

Behind the monument the track ends and we head uphill to the beacon without a path. Behind it are traces of the island's most recent history. The builders came from Germany, as can be deciphered on the blasted concrete of the
0.20 **bunkers** from 1943.

In the north you see a rocky hilltop [1]. Heading in this direction diagonally without a path, later below a cliff face (right), you traverse a ditch. Up on a plateau you come, 50m to the right of the broken-down walls, to a 30m long Stone Age workshop [2] (**P1:** N 36°43.363'/E 24°25.956'). Here black obsidian, a compact glassy rock which forms a crust on lava streams, was extracted and transported away on ships. The stone was made into tools and weapons on board and sold later.

Turning your back on the sea, make your way up the fall
0.35 line to the **enclosed ground** with even greater amounts of obsidian. This largest find on Milos is called **Nýchia** ("Nails"). It is believed that obsidian was mined here for 8000 years. Mílos was one of the earliest Cycladic islands to be inhabited, with traces going back as far as the 3rd millennium BC.

Going round the fenced field, you find tracks on the other
0.50 side leading inland to the **dirt track** (**P2:** N43°689'/E24°26.028', 100m) which could have been used as an alternative way here.

Now go left, past a shed (right), bearing right at a fork and
0.55 walk towards Tripití and reach the **rural chapel** of Saint Antonius, with olive tree (**P3:** N36°43.389'/E24°25.944').

> ***Alternative:*** The second half of the following route to Klíma is pathless, partly leading through tallish scrub. You can avoid it by continuing straight ahead and

then descending along the road to Klíma.
Savour the sea view though on a short detour to the chapel of Klimatovoúni.

0.55 Otherwise behind the Antonius chapel a wall-lined dirt track bears left. Running behind the solar plant (right) past a farmhouse (right) with vineyard, it leads between vegetable fields above the sea and on to picture-book
1.00 **olive tree terraces** (p. 145). On the other side of the huge
★ bay towers the mountain of the Prophet and down below the ferries bring in holidaymakers, the new conquerors of the island.

Having torn yourself away from the beautiful view, you climb down five metres and follow the terrace, along which a mule track leads further north. Where the terraces end, you have to climb over low walls and should then keep uphill rather than downhill. The terraces continue here too, though they are now covered with scrub. Soon you catch sight of the fishing village of Klíma below. When going down through the phrýgana, it is advisable to keep right on the mountain as the slopes drop away steeply! Above the houses the track becomes even steeper
1.20 and overgrown with trees, until you reach the **road.** Next to the restaurant "Panorama" you climb down a narrow
1.25 path to the picturesque **harbour of Klima.**

At the far end take the alley inland for 20m and then turn left immediately behind the chapel on to a steep stepped path. It converges with a wide kalderími, which brings
1.35 you up to the two thick walls of **Old Melos.** There you turn sharp right to the theatre.

The city was inhabited from 1000 BC to 1000 AD. It was founded by the Dorians, who had previously destroyed Fy-

lakopí. Later the Romans also erected buildings on the site. The recently restored theatre [4] was built in the Hellenistic period (300 BC) and used for 200 years. It was built of marble which had to be transported to the volcanic island of Milos. The present-day capacity is only 1/10 of the former 7,000 seats.

You return the same way, then up right and, above the walls, up the paved track to a plateau with a kind of "turning place", over which are scattered ancient building parts. The detour to the right leads on the roadway alongside the site of the "Venus of Milo" (right), the statue now on display in the Louvre. Then go right 120m down the
1.40 road to the **catacombs.**

This underground cemetery, the largest in Greece, was secretly laid out by the Christian community from the 1st to the 6th century AD. 7000 to 8000 dead lie buried here. Three chambers can be visited on guided tours. They are closed on Mondays.

Go back up the approach road, turn left in the right bend and return to the "turning place". There you will find a
1.50 path going right, which soon **forks.**

Alternatives: On the left a path leads to the summit chapel of **Profítis Elias** where, in Roman times, an Apollo temple used to stand.

At a fork below the hill it is possible to go right, down to the place where Roman villas were found. After eight minutes you come to a few columns on the left. Significant floor mosaics were discovered here, but they had to be covered up again as a means of protection.

1.50 The path widens as it joins the ascending kalderími,
1.55 which reaches **Pláka** in a transversal alley. Go left up some steps, left again at the following alley, left yet again 5m afterwards and then straight ahead on the flat. Having passed *Betty's Studios* (left), you walk straight uphill at the fork, then right up and horizontally to the left. To be absolutely sure, though, it is advisable to ask for the
2.00 **Panagía Korfiatíssa** ("the" sunset rendezvous).

If you proceed straight on from there and continue to the right for another 15 minutes at the fork, you come to the kástro. The Venetians ruled the island from this fortress from 1207 until 1566.

A perfect way to end a day steeped in history or, for the

sake of it, you can visit the very well appointed museum (closed Mondays).

Hikers with stamina could end up by joining ㊸ down to a nice beach!

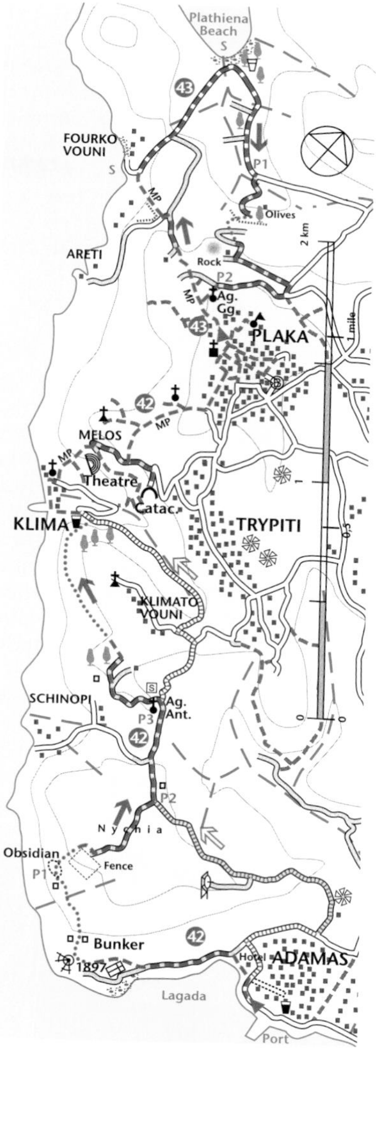

㊸ Sunset

The most famous place to enjoy the sunset is of course the wall in front of Panagía Korfiatíssa church in Pláka. Those who would rather experience the spectacle alone, however, should undertake this 2-hour circular trek and remember to take their bathing-trunks. And not forget to have a sundowner either.

■ 5 km, difference in altitude 170m, easy

▷ *Map see previous page*

AWT From the round apse at the rear of the **Panagía church**
0.00 stroll left, left again at the end of the alley and into an alley with inns which later widens. From the palm continue straight ahead on the wide street, which divides after a few metres. A sign points right up to the kástro.
If you go *down left,* you immediately find a kalderími leading out of this beautiful town. The path soon forks – we
0.05 go right. On the right-hand side you notice **whitewashed steps**, indicating a path going right to St. George's chapel. We continue straight on downhill, cross a dirt track and are not at all pleased that from here on the old footpath
0.10 has been replaced by a **roadway.**
At the next turn-off after two minutes (with power line) you go left for 30m. In front of the sharp-angled garden wall of a holiday complex you turn off right and saunter down a kalderími to the fishing village of **Fourkovoúni** 1. If you do not wish to bathe between the normally unoccupied beach cottages, follow the dirt track up to the

right. At the next fork you head down for the white **sandy**
beach of Pláthienas, where you find an open cantina in
0.25 summer. If this spot is really to your liking, you can cele-
brate the sunset here and arrange to be picked up by a
taxi.

Short cut: The track described below runs through thick undergrowth for about 100m. So for the return leg you could take the already familiar trail and further up at the white steps take the path left to St. George's chapel.

Otherwise you march on up the asphalt road from the
0.25 **beach** for 8 minutes. After the second left-hand bend of
the street (at the third right turn-off), you turn off right at
0.35 the **power line** (**P1:** N36°45.043'/E24°25.028'). Having
taken a dirt track across the valley bottom, you walk up to
an olive grove with a white shed.

Proceeding right through the grove and across the terraces, you climb over a low field wall. Keeping immediately to the right of this wall, you now make your way up through the undergrowth without a path in the direction of the prominent rock. Above the grove you cross a dirt track and climb a further 30m in the same direction with-
out a path. Below the prominent rock you later meet the
0.45 **dirt track** again, which you go up. Beside a barn (right)
0.50 you follow the dirt track to the left to the **road**, but leave
this again after 5m by joining a dirt track on the right.

Gradually climbing up this track, you have vertiginous wooden balconies hanging above you on the kástro hill on the left and a distant view of the sea, dominated by the island of Antimílos, on the right.

At a sort of fork (**P2:** N36°44.808'/E24°25.222') you pro-
1.00 ceed left up to the cave chapel **Agios Geórgios** [2]. Inside it
is half natural, half man-made. In front lies the small resting place for that private sunset we were promised ...

In front of this spot is a path which will bring you back to
the already familiar kalderími and up left to **Pláka**, where
1.05 the crowd of sun-worshipers has now disappeared.

 Sérifos, Livádi with Chóra

Sérifos

Sérifos is relatively mountainous and sometimes appears to be barren, its name meaning "infertile". Stretching across the middle of the island is an elongated massif consisting of granite and gneiss, where the highest peak, Troúlos, reaches the formidable height of 582m. The western side drops more steeply down to the sea than the eastern side, where the chóra built half way up the mountain looks down on pleasantly green slopes and beautiful sandy beaches.
On weekends many Athenians occupy the hotel beds in Livádi. Otherwise the island is not overrun, being just the place for hikers in search of tranquillity. In the hinterland it still offers a few old and now marked tracks, numerous wells and one of the most exciting kalderími on the Cyclades (see left). Walks 44 and 46 are specially recommended.
Hiking maps: Anavasi #10.25/Terrain # 303/Nakas Road #107
Taxis: +30-693 243 1114 / 697 380 1051

44 The monastery of the archangels

The most famous sight on Sérifos is the Moní ton Taxiarchón, an over 400-year old fortified monastery. It is one of the goals of the 8-hour hike, for which you need to be fit. So you should do like the pilgrims and rise early. Along the way are plenty of springs, but no tavernas.
■ *16 km, difference in altitude 205 m, difficult*

1

2

AWT At the little square above the **bus stop in the Chóra** stock
0.00 up with edibles, then set off to the left of kafeníon ΜΥΛΟΙ,
"Mills", down a few concrete steps, right on the concrete
path and then immediately left down the hill. A paved
path leads to a group of houses and then out into the
0.05 open countryside. At the **first right-hand bend** you go
straight ahead on the path marked "1", and again at the
following fork. Head for the mountains which are
"crowned" by two antennae.
0.10 The trail drops into a hollow with an old **stone bridge** [1],
beside which the first well is waiting (**P1:** N37°27.793'/
E24°25.542'). Sérifos is proud of its allegedly one hundred
wells and today we can test a few of them. Climb up from
the bridge, following the path. On the crest of the hill is
St. Stephen's chapel (right) and a house. On the other side
of the dirt track you go into the next valley and on to the
0.20 next **bridge.** Not nearly as elegant as the first one, yet un-
!! mistakable on account of its *curved steel railings.*
Then you walk along a sunken path. When the lateral
0.25 walls come to an end, you should watch out: A **trail** cross-
es here imperceptibly! (**P2:** N 37°10.111'/ E 24°30.402')
Go left, following the "1". (㊺ leads straight on).
Passing some ruins (left), later on a dirt track, you come
0.35 up to the flat-roofed **Páno Stavrós chapel** with blue bell-
tower [2]. As the name suggests, this is the "upper" cruci-
form chapel, as well as having been a crossroads at the
same time. It is so pleasantly cool inside, even providing a
small table, that one is in absolutely no hurry to leave the
semi-darkness again.
The charming trail continues behind the chapel. Hugging
the edge of the hill, you can refresh your geography of the

Cyclades: Sífnos, Kímolos, Mílos – from left or right? The
0.50 skilfully laid kalderími leads past a **pen** (right) before becoming an overgrown gravel track.
1.00 From the **saddle** (**P3:** N37°10.753′/E24°30.889, 375m) you look down upon Kéndarchos, according to the islanders the prettiest village. That is why it is also called kallítsos, “the most beautiful one”.

> ***Alternative:*** If you want to walk via Kéndarchos, descend until you find a footpath leading first to the hamlet Kámpos, then running parallel to the road for a bit. But from the Skopianí church you have to take it for 20 minutes.

Otherwise you climb up the branching off roadway from
1.00 the **saddle** and come to a wider **roadway;** where it curves,
1.05 you turn off right. Almost on the same level you proceed to a saddle occupied by a villa. From there the roadway runs downhill, at the end with a concrete surface. The im-
1.30 pressive **Taxiarchón Monastery** (230m) [3] is situated down to the right. Once on the **road,** take a look to see if the little blue door is closed. If so, even hard knocking will be to no avail.

> *The somewhat elderly Monk Makários (p. 3) takes care of the monastery. The tiny portal, which used only to be accessible via a ladder, is protected by a machicolation. The 10m high fortified monastery dates from the 15th century and has 60 rooms, which are picturesquely grouped round the church. It once accommodated 30 monks and 30 lay brethren. In the church of the Saints Michael and Gabriel, Makários proudly shows the dazzling altar screen made of marble and the gold-plated wood carving with a wonderful icon by the famous artist Skordilis.*

3

4

On the road go left at the fork to the bus stop (departure approx. 3.20 pm). Concrete steps lead downhill; this is the local trekking route "6". Soon you arrive in Galaní ("the sky-blue one"), a sloping village in the centre of which stands a church with a modern concrete cross. The inhabitants used to earn a living from keeping silkworms. You may be lucky and find a kafeníon that is open.

Walking horizontally, then down steps as far as a power line and turning left there on the same level, you cross the village and come to the access road on the other side. Go up this for about 120m and then turn right on to narrow
1.45 **path** (**P4:** N37°11.383'/E24°26.760', 230m). Route "6" leads you along the edge of the slope, above the valley bottom with dovecotes on your right. In the hollow with thick oleander bushes you cross a concrete retaining wall and then the beautiful, narrow path starts to ascend
2.00 again. Where it forks, head right up to a **dirt track** (**P5:** N37°11.122'/E24°29.925').

30m further to the left you again go uphill, past Polikarpos chapel (left) and a farmhouse with a water tap in the garden. The two friendly occupants are glad to see visitors. From there steps made of lumps of rock lead further uphill, before forking *right*. In the saddle you pass the
2.10 Sotiras chapel. 15m beyond where a **dirt track** begins (**P6:** N37°11.019'/E24°29.778') you turn off to the left and
2.20 continue on up the fall line to the **road.** Here you could stop the afternoon bus.

Across the road are concrete steps which bring you through the deserted hamlet **Pírgos** ("tower"). 20m below the chapel turn left and walk down a monopáti to a large well above the road.

A welcome pit stop before the final ascent of the day, which starts right behind the well (**P7:** N37°10.766'/E24°29.866', 360m). Once more giving of your best, you initially climb below the fence (right), later to the right of the facing fence or wall on an indistinct path up through boulders and proudly look down on Galaní. Higher up you climb right on to a level area. Without a path, immediately to the right of a fence, you proceed across this area and then, in front of the bending off fence, to the right
2.35 until below the antenna you reach a **roadway** (**P8:** N37° 10.690'/E24°30.154). Standing on the right is a holiday house.

The trail into the opposite valley is overgrown, forcing us to use the roadway on the left. In the saddle (470m) be sure first to enjoy the distant view of the sea, possibly even discovering Páros.

3.00 The descent leads to a **left-hand bend** (**P9:** N37°10.748'/ E24°30.717') and then right, down a rather overgrown roadway, to P3, from where you again see Kéndarchos.

3.25 Take the already familiar kalderími right to the **Páno Stavrós Chapel.**

There you descend the roadway which starts down below, but at once turn off right on to a path running up through the hollow with the curved railings to the St.

3.45 **Stephan's Chapel** (left).

From there you go right, up a roadway, and, where it forks, left. 50m after the right-hand bend you find a well-beaten track on the left, which further up leads through a

★ gap in the wall. You are rewarded with a fabulous view of Chóra [4]. Lost in reverie, you wander between the ter-

4.00 races, traverse a trough with a **well** and arrive in **Chóra.**

4.10 Phew, we have certainly earned a drink now, but no water please this time.

Feast-Days – Panigíri

Often the hiker is fortunate enough to land completely unexpectedly in the middle of a religious festival. The church or chapel is bedecked with flags, a large congregation of guests in festive dress is sitting around – in their midst at least one priest. The tables are groaning under the weight of the food which the womenfolk or the owner of a private chapel have brought with them. Home-made drinks are offered; canned drinks are sold at cost price. Immediately the stranger is invited to taste the many dishes and is involved in a conversation. These are unforgettable Greek moments. The festivals take place on the name day of the patron saint:

23rd April	Áyios Geórgios	20th July	Profítis Ilías
5th May	Ayía Iríni	26th July	Ayía Paraskeví
21st May	Áyios Konstantínos	27th July	Áyios Panteleímon
Ascension Day	Ayía Análipsi	6th August	Metamórphosis
Whitsuntide	Ayía Triáda	15th August	Assumption of the Virgin
24th June	Ay. Ioánnis Pródomos	29th August	Áyios Ioánnis
29th June	Ayíi Apóstoli	1st Sept.	Áyios Mámas
7th July	Ayía Kyriakí	14th Sept.	Áyios Stavrós

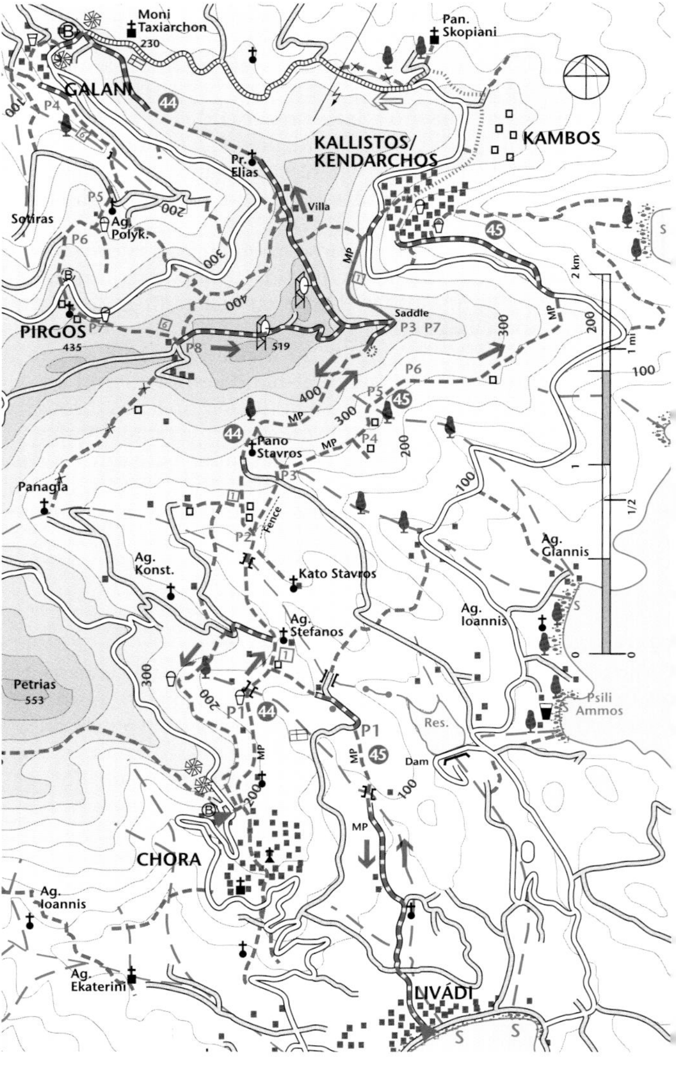
Moni
Taxiarchon
230
Pan.
Skopiani
GALANI
KALLISTOS/
KENDARCHOS
KAMBOS
Pr.
Elias
Villa
Sotiras
Ag.
Polyk.
PIRGOS
435
519
Saddle
Pano
Stavros
Panagia
Ag.
Konst.
Kato Stavros
Ag.
Stefanos
Ag.
Giannis
Ag.
Ioannis
Petrias
553
Psili
Ammos
Res.
Dam
CHORA
Ag.
Ioannis
Ag.
Ekaterini
LIVÁDI
Fence
2 km
1 mi

㊺ Kallítsos, the prettiest village

This 7-hour walk on the unspoilt eastern side of the island leads along old, yet easily identifiable paths to Kéndarchos, also called Kallítsos, "prettiest village". The tracks are still used by farmers, but are not marked. So one should have a certain "eye for paths" - or at least for red dots. Once there, you could take a bus at 3.10 pm. Because there is nowhere to stop off, food for the journey is a must. Kallítsos has two wells.

■ 7,5 km, difference in altitude 250m, moderate to difficult

▷ *map see left*

AWT From the middle of **Livádi** strand, 50m to the right of the
0.00 **restaurant ΣΤΑΜΑΤΗΣ,** next to the sign "Amalia", a dirt
road runs inland. We follow it, past smallish holiday
0.10 houses, as far as a **hollow** covered with reeds. Standing
there on the right behind an electricity metre is a dovecote. Immediately after that you go left up along concrete, pass two large holiday houses on the left and head for the hill crowned by rocks resembling ruins. Beneath
0.20 this hill is a concrete **bridge** beside more dovecotes [1].
It now takes eight minutes along a rocky track to reach a
0.30 **roadway** (**P1:** N37°09.616'/E24°30.747, 120m), which
you follow up to the right and, *already after 40m, left.* To the left of the roadway is a water tank. 100m above the bridge in the dip, continue straight ahead at the fork, past a small farmhouse (right) until you discover an almost

forgotten monopáti. This track leads up to a fork beside a ruin (right), where you go right (marking "1", also the route of ㊹).

0.40 Walk right up this path to **St. Stephen's chapel** and a house. In the next little green valley are a solitary chape
0.45 up on the right and further down a **bridge** with *curve steel railings*. Beyond the following, deeply sunken path
0.50 our route **leaves** that of ㊹, which runs left up to Stavró chapel (**P2:** N37°10.111'/E24°30.402').

On the left of a wire mesh fence you go *straight ahead* and
0.55 come – latterly on a monopáti – to a **saddle** (245m) with a fine view over Psilí Ammos bathing bay.

After going straight across a dirt track there (**P3** N37°10.291'/E24°499'/E24°30.499', 235m), you descend
1.00 through a **gorge** covered with oleander bushes ②. Regaining height, your panorama extends from Sífnos as far distant Páros. Do not take the path right down towards the
1.10 sea at a **fork** (**P4:** N37°10.419'/E24°30.723', 240m), but continue straight ahead, keeping to the contour lines. Be-
1.15 side **house ruins** (right) the path swings left and, afte
1.20 100m, leads through a gully ③ (**P5:** N37°10.530'/E24 30.811', 230m). From there proceed up through bizarre boulders, always heading for the distant slopes.
1.25 Beyond the rocks you find a gently ascending **mule path** (**P6:** N37°10.602'/E24°30.934'). On the right-hand side o
1.30 the first foothill is a **hut** (250m), after the second one you can look down into the Kéndarchos valley. The high-lying village of Kallítsos was built to be safe from marauding pirates. The unplastered houses at that time were stone-grey and therefore hardly visible from the sea.
1.45 Further down the path joins the **road** near the power line

Cross it 50m over to the left and then take the roadway downhill ④. (If you want to head for the pebble beach, walk along the road towards the sea until you find a path down.)

Keeping to the left, you soon approach the village and discover a wayside well with clear water, the former washing place. At the fork at the lower edge of the village you
amble straight ahead to the steps and on up to beautiful
2.00 **Kéndarchos-Kallítsos.** The main alley here also has a well
and an inviting resting place. Only a handful of inhabitants have stayed in the village.

From the well follow the sign "1" to the left/west and use
2.05 the steps to the **road.** Walk along this for about 120m until you come to the paved path running uphill. Having gone up this, walk past where the roadway turns off to the right (**P7:** N37°10.753'/E24°30.889', 390m). The Chóra in
sight again, you head towards it gently descending the
2.40 kalderími as far as the **Apáno Stavrós chapel.**

Below the chapel go 100m along the roadway and turn off right on to a path.

> ***Alternative:*** The roadway leads in 35 minutes to the popular sandy beach of Psilí Amos with tavernas!

The fork **P2** from this morning is reached in no time, go
3.00 right there, on through the defile and to the **curved rail-**
3.05 **ings.** Further up at **St. Stephan's chapel** (left) one could
3.40 take this morning's trail straight on to **Livádi.** In doing
so, do not overlook the indistinct turn-off after 100m at the ruin (left)!

Alternatively one can follow the description on page 165
3.30 to the **Chóra.**

㊻ View of the chóra

The 4-hour trek leads on lanes and paths, including one of the most amazing cobblestone paths, from the mountain village of Panagiá over the Troúlos ridge to the chóra of Sérifos.
The route does not offer any wells and the only kafenía is back in the chóra.
■ ***10 km, difference in altitude 330m, moderate***

AWT Drive to **Panagiá** (340m) by bus or taxi (€ 14.–) and go down steps into the pretty village.

The Our Lady's Chapel with red tiles is the oldest on the island. Alas the 600 year old frescos (the Last Supper on the right) are hardly recognizable any more. The owner of the café at the car park has the key.
A bawdy dance used to be held round the olive tree in front of the chapel to decide which couple would marry first. Those were the days!

0.00 Opposite the **chapel** the sign with the sturdy wayfarer shows us reality and the way to tour "4". We follow. At once we go right and after six meters – at the *bevelled corner of the house* – left. At the street light beside the power pole we go up left, following the "4". Then at the next pole up steps to a short, level stretch of path. After two minutes we leave the village downhill.
The trail runs below disused terraces 1 more or less on the same level. Down below lies Sikamía bay, behind it the island of Kíthnos. In the region of Vatsamo you pass a spring (left) and a washing area in a green oblique dip. Three minutes later the trail "4" turns up left at a right an-

gle – if you want to save 35 minutes of walking.
Otherwise you continue straight ahead on the same level,
.30 following the path to the right in a **cross-gully.** Dotted across the abandoned terraced cornfields in the valley are a few dovecotes. Where the path forks, you go on up left
.40 as far as the **Panagía Kamarotí chapel** [2]. A delightful spot.

Those in need of a training session can dash up the steep path across the rocky crest behind the chapel. The slower walker enjoys the same view from the gently ascending
.50 roadway. At the **turn-off** into the valley you go up left to the Panagía Roudianí chapel [3] with formidable panorama view over to the monastery of Saint Thekla on the peak.

.00 At a goat pen you are re-joined by **trail "4"**. Then the roadway climbs more steeply and has a concrete surface. 250m after it ends – after two turn-offs – our trail "4" turns *to the left* at a pole.

Initially it runs across open terrain, where you should watch out for markings. Then it is lined by walls for a
.25 short section; after the **crest** (550m) it follows the electricity cables downhill. Beyond where the helipad appears,
.35 you cross the **fork** in the direction of same until you come to a right-hand bend.

There you find the path marked "2", which later leads
.50 down right to a wall-lined path. Soon you reach the **St. George's chapel**, from where you have one of the most exciting panoramas on the Cyclades: a bird's eye view of the chóra of Sérifos, behind that the small island Vous [4]. Then you have the pleasure of taking one of the most beautiful kalderími which you will find anywhere nowa-

days (p. 161). It was laboriously constructed to connect the ore mines around Méga Livádi with Chóra. It is only when strolling down it that one appreciates the builders' colossal achievement, happily pausing for a minute's silence before proceeding past the
2.10 windmills to **Chóra** (220m).

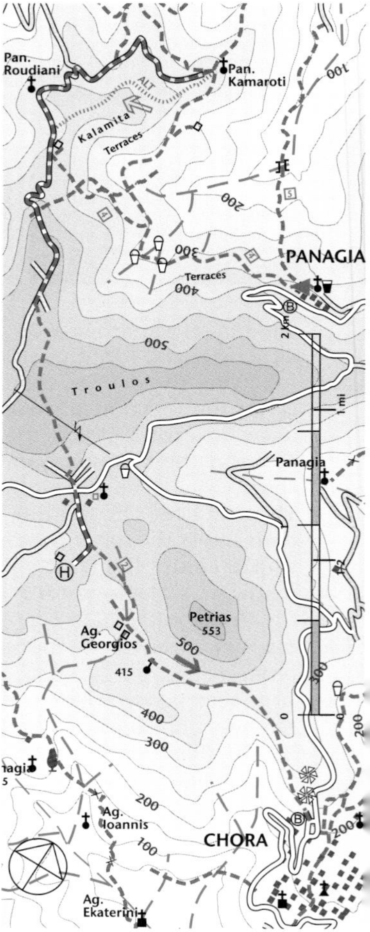

47 Cape Spathí beacon

A straightforward, 3½-hour coastal walk. At the end of the treeless trail you can expect a beacon and some sunbathing on steep cliffs. No tavernas or springs.
■ 10 km, difference in altitude 160m, easy

ꟼWT
).00 In **Livádi** head inland at the wayside altar next to the yacht jetty. Having stocked up with the bare essentials at the clutch of stores, you take the road straight ahead past the school sports field (right) over the hill, mostly alongside empty holiday houses. To your left lies Livadákia beach, which you can enjoy at the finish.

).15 The road later leads through **Rámos**, where you veer left at the manifold beside the electricity pole and come to the village chapel. Ignore this and the turn-off, too. Ditto a roadway which descends from the right. March straight on through a small dip with the old village washing area (right).

Further up you see the crossing which you will encounter again on the way back. Here you turn down left and, at
).20 the (closed) **left turn-off**, follow the electricity poles up the hill. (The left turn-off shortly before the saddle is marked on the island maps as a path to Alevrákia beach. But it can only be identified for the first six minutes, thereafter one has to walk "by eye".)

).25 On the **saddle** it is now possible to see the beacon, with Alevrákia bay on the left. In the distance Sífnos awaits us. In the next bay is an aquafarm, to which the roadway leads. Already before the electricity poles we therefore

1

2

0.40 leave it by going **right** on slabs of rock and find a mule track running over the mountain ridge. It ends at the dri-
0.55 veway leading to **Spathí beacon,** built in 1901 [1]. To the right of it a path drops to slabs of rock on which it is possible to "splash about" endlessly. Once back up at
1.05 the **beacon** you begin the ascent on the roadway leading
1.20 to the **road.**

Alternative: The route which is now described affords marvellous sea panoramas, albeit along asphalt for a quarter of an hour. It may hence be preferable to return the same way.

1.20 On the **road** you climb right a little before descending into
1.35 a dip with a large **agricultural enterprise.** It is best to go right up the roadway between walls and round the hill to a new olive grove (right), where a monopáti commences with a fine view of the Chóra. Walking past a farmhouse, you again reach the
1.50 **crossing** from the outward leg. Take the already familiar way as far as the chapel, but this time turn off 50m after it. Then immediately left and, at the narrow alley, descend right to a car park. There, in front of holiday houses, is a roadway which takes you right at a T-junction down to the sea. At the bottom you turn left in front of an
2.00 **enclosure** and arrive at the tree-lined sandy beach of
2.10 **Livadákia** [2], where you can relax after the tour …

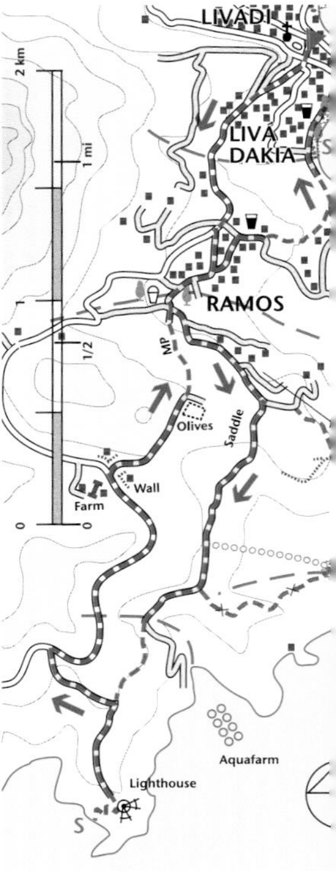

Síkinos

Long overlooked by tourism, the island is gradually catching up, now possessing numerous well appointed rooms in addition to the fair-sized selection of harbour tavernas. Since the island does not have a daily ferry service, it still offers tranquil island life.
It is supplied with sufficient water from a number of springs. Most of the original mule tracks are preserved, because the 240 permanent inhabitants are also content with fewer new roads: a trekking island of the highest order, walks 48 and 49 are specially recommended. Sadly parts of these may have been affected by the fire in early September 2015!
Hiking maps: Anavasi #10.29 / Terrain # 317

48 A lonely path

Not a soul in sight for a couple of hours ... Anyone keen to have such an experience will find regions behind Kástro and Apáno Chorió where neither man nor beast will cross their path.
From Kástro (= AWT 1.05) the shortened tour takes 5 hours, from Aloprónia 6 to 7. The route almost entirely follows old monopátia. There is a good well. For this most impressive walk certain path-finding skills are required.
■ *12 km, difference in altitude 410m, difficult*

AWT From the **beach** in **Aloprónia** you go up the road to the
0.00 **petrol station**, there up right towards Pirgári and further
0.05 up until you reach the right-hand bend in the concrete
0.07 road. On the left is the **reservoir** (**P1:** N36°40.942'/
E25°08.569'), and to the right of it begins a rocky
0.20 monopáti. Climbing gradually, it passes **barns** (left) below
a chapel. Further on is a well on the right-hand side.
Having later walked 40m up the road, you find a short
stretch of paved path on the left. Then a further 80m of
0.30 **asphalt** until, between the antenna (left) and a taverna, a
roadway begins. After dropping slowly, it rises to the
0.45 charmingly furnished **Blasius Chapel.**
Here begins a kalderími which runs uphill to the right of
the ditch, goes round a bend and ends at wide steps lead-
1.05 ing up to **Kástro bus stop.**
To the left of the chapel at the bus stop more steps lead up
1.10 to the "upper village", **Apáno Chório.** At the chapel with
two semi-domes on the lower outskirts you go up right
through the sleepy, tightly clustered village. Markings "1"
and "2".
At the end of the village you find a stair-path, which affords views of the sea on the other side of the island. The bizarre building with pinnacles down on the road was the residence of the Italian commander of the island in the war. The scene is characterized by a whole group of islands, dominated by Zeus, the highest peak on Náxos. At 1004m, also the highest in the Cyclades.
The upper part of the village consists entirely of the ruins
of houses. Ascending the steps between these, you stum-
1.20 ble over the round stump of a **windmill.**
Behind it the old trail leads on up in the direction of the Paraskeví chapel at the top of the mountain. At the fork below that though do not follow the markings, but go right (**P2:** N36°41.422'/E25°06.822').
We relish the wonderful path which meanders along the
1.30 side of the slope and brings us to the deserted hamlet **Sta-
matiní** (**P3:** N 36°41. 318'/ E 25°06.463'). Going round
the lowest house, you go downhill at the fork, soon sight-
ing a double chapel [1]. Ignore the turn-off to the right,
1.40 but not the **well** on the left a little further on, with its
crystal-clear water.
Attention: *The stretch as far as the sea was affected by a fire in September 2015. However the old description which follows*

should apply again after the winter rains.
Twenty metres beyond the well you turn right at the fork on the slabs of rock and go downhill. A magnificent rock path now begins [2]. Over to the left on the counterslope a deserted settlement, down in the valley round cisterns. The trail follows the contours, ascending gradually.
As might be expected in such a bleak region, you discover
2.05 a round **refuge** further up and later, below a huge cairn, a
2.10 **second refuge** (**P4:** N36°40.713'/E25°07.218').
Over towards the sea rises a cone-shaped mountain (379m) whose right-hand slopes we will later use for the descent. On the slopes you pass a large round stone pen and to the right of it you come to a track which keeps left above the valley.
2.35 Quite far down in the valley you later come across **ruined houses** by the wayside. Soon after you notice a small house on the left-hand side of the counterslope. To the right above our track stands a dry-stone wall (**P5:**
!! N36°39.849'/E25°07.171'). Here you turn *left down into the*
2.45 **valley bottom.** (You can tell you have gone too far and have to turn back if you see the Panteleimon chapel on your right after three minutes.)
Climbing up the other side of the valley, you pass a dried-up well on the left and walk straight on, later going through a cleft in the rock. Over on the right on the oppo-
3.00 site slope stands the Panteleimon chapel. From the **saddle** you then see the port of Aloprónia. From there down you stroll across broad terraced cornfields until you come to a
3.20 **dirt track** which leads you effortlessly along the shoreline
3.35 to **Aloprónia.**

Adverse effects of the island fire on 6th and 7th September 2015: According to research the area was closed. The author asks for field reports, which he will gladly make known!

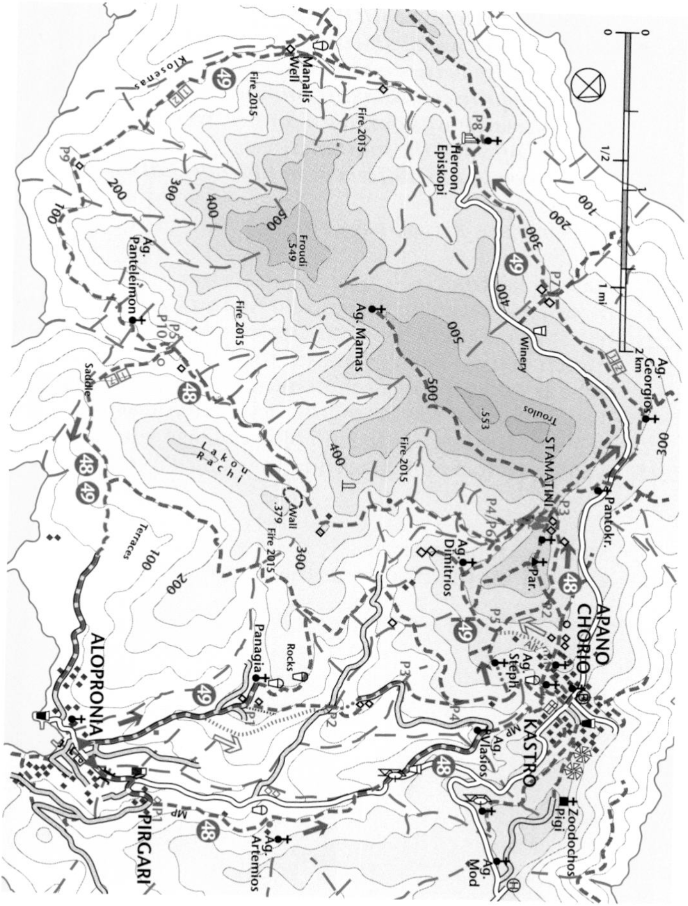

49 Our Lady's Church in the temple

This 7 or 9½-hour circular tour can be started in Kástro or Aloprónia and leads to the island's most important archaeological site – a Roman marble sepulchral temple –, which is sadly closed. But it also has a few landscape highlights in store. Particularly enchanting is the initial stretch as far as Heróon temple, which the locals call Episkopí. Walking almost entirely on mule tracks, we pass a number of wells, albeit sometimes without a pail. On the leg between Manali's well and the sea you will require certain path-finding skills. In early 2015 this section was damaged for fire, which may also have affected the markings.
■ *14 or 16 km, difference in altitude 390 m, difficult*

▷ *map see previous page*

AWT **Start in Kástro:**
0.00 In **Kástro**, you go up the steps to **Apáno Chorió** from the bus stop on the left of the chapel. In front of the first church you go straight ahead, then up the steps to the right as far as the next church (right). From here you always leave one row of houses between yourself and the fields on the left. At the end of the village you find steps
0.15 leading on to a mule track and the point **P5** (=AWT 1.25).

Start in Aloprónia:
0.00 Go 80m up the road from the bridge at the strand and

turn on to the first dirt track at the transformer station leading steeply up to the left.

0.15 ***Short cut:*** To avoid the last climb up to the church, you could make a short cut by turning off to the right on to a track 50m after the signpost.

Otherwise you later disregard a turn-off to the left and come further up, after ruins and a field wall, to the de-
0.25 lightfully situated **Panagía Church.** On 5th September 2015 a small fire in front of the door [1] got out of control and devastated half the island.

Walk back 120m from the church until you find a goat
!! track going to the *left two metres in front of the field wall* (**P1:** N36°40.934'/E25°07.995', 190m). To the left of the
0.40 wall this takes you into the **valley** and across a sandy track. On the other side (**P2:** N36°41.148'/E25°07.798, 110m) you climb up on the left-hand side of rocky ledges.
0.45 At the top you use a **dirt track**, from which later a **path**
0.50 leads up left in the right-hand bend in a dip (**P3:** N36°41.249'/E25°07.514') and through a charming, typi-
1.00 cally Greek landscape until it joins a **horizontal path** (**P4:** N36°41.428'/E25°07.423', 215m).

Go right here, turning *left 50m after a small house (right)*
1.10 on to a path **leading uphill** between high walls. This path
1.15 later **peters out**, though, so you climb up to **Agios**
1.20 **Stephános chapel** without a path. A stupendous picnic spot awaits you there!

From here a path runs uphill; go past the left-hand turn-off after 100m. At the T-junction further up you come to a
1.25 **monopáti** running along the side of the hill and walk left. (You would have come from the right had you taken the short cut from Kástro.)

At the next fork you go up right ("7"), at the next one down left. Then one could take a detour down left to the
1.30 solitary **Agios Dimítrios chapel**, also a nice spot for a picnic.

Up on the main trail walk to the end of the valley. Further
1.35 down is an ill defined **fork** (**P6:** N36°41.161'/E25°06.797'), where walk 48 drops down to the left – today we go up to the right and after a few metres pass a well (right). Now go
1.45 straight uphill to the deserted hamlet **Stamatiní.**

From there you proceed down a track to the Pantokrator
1.50 chapel at the **road.** Walk left up it for 150m, where a large sign indicates the "old path"; we gladly follow this and

1.55 soon come to the **St. George's chapel** (right).
We now ramble up and down between abandoned ter-
★ raced cornfields, Folégandros to our right. Be sure to take
time to savour the landscape [2]. Up on the left are the ter-
races of the "winery" (evenings only). There follows a de-
scent into a ditch with a turn-off, but you go uphill and
2.15 pass some **ruins** (left), between which a path leads uphill
(**P7:** N36°40.628'/E25°05.809, 315m).
Here you proceed straight ahead, then climb again. **Be-**
2.25 **low the road** are markings to the right which lead you
along a monopáti, appropriately enough, to Heróon – al-
2.30 so called **Episkopí** [3] (**P8:** N36°40.175'/E25°05.542').

3000 years ago this lonely region was the site of an ancient Ionian city, whose acropolis stood on the mountain now crowned by the Agía Marína chapel. Down here were the necropolises, the most important of which was the Heróon, the marble tomb of a noble family; two crypts still remain. In the 5th century AD it was converted into Our Lady's Church, integrating the ground plan and the entrance façade into the new structure. In 1688 the church became Episkopí monastery, whose cells and embrasures are still partly preserved.

Coming away from this impressive place, you return along the familiar path for 200m, but then turn right downhill.

Attention: *The fire in early September 2015 also affected this valley as far down as the sea!*

Instead of schist you soon feel marble slabs beneath your
2.45 feet [4]. Up to the right of the path stands a **small house.**
Describing a right-hand bend round the mountain, the
3.00 path eventually brings you to **Manali's well.**

Further down, after two or three minutes, you come to a
!! slab of rock, from where you go *left* through a small wall
and then across the valley. After passing the ruins of some
houses (right), you proceed along rather overgrown
!! tracks, *keeping to the left of the valley bottom,* towards the
sea. Be careful not to lose sight of the trail!
At the sea (**P9:** N36°39.210′/E25°06.732′) the path turns
3.35 off to the left 15m below some **ruins.** Again it starts off
rather overgrown. You pass a tall rocky needle (right) and,
4.00 round the bend, come to **Agios Panteleímon chapel**,
which provides a "divine" resting place.
Continuing on along the slope, you go right after three or
four minutes (**P10:** N36°39.849′/E 25°07.171′), down into
4.05 the **valley bottom.** This corresponds to **P5** on walk 48.
5.00 Now follow that description as far as **Aloprónia.**

▶ **Lodging on the waterside** is possible at the delightful pension Lucas in Aloprónia (tel. 22860 51076)

50 Naval review

This pleasant, 6-hour walk through charming scenery leads along marvellous mule tracks and ends up at the famous monastery Zoodóchos Pigi, the monastery of the "life-giving source". Along the way hikers can also refresh themselves at a real source.

■ 10 km, difference in altitude 80m, moderate

AWT Starting point is the obelisk on the Platía in **Kástro.** The
0.00 closely interlocking medieval Venetian kástro used to stand here, but was pulled down during the Italian occupation.

Proceed along the left-hand side of the church, then left and left again into the next alleyway with two cafés. Then up left in front of the bakery and immediately right. Situated on the left of the alley is the forecourt of St. Catherine's church [1]. After that comes a fork. Left leads up to the monastery – we go right here (**P1:** N36°40.942'/E25°08.570') on the horizontal paved track and leave the village to the right with a cheerful heart.

At the fork above the antenna and chapel you go left, with views over to the island Ios, until you reach the road
0.25 in front of **Agios Modestos chapel**, with barrel-vaulted roof.
0.30 Take the road up as far as the **right-hand bend** below the helipad. 50m after the bend, still ahead of the level land-
!! fill site, you turn off left on the same level on to an *indistinct* roadway (**P2:** N36°41.987'/E25°07.973'). A track
!! branches off to the right after 400m at a *cairn* (**P3:**

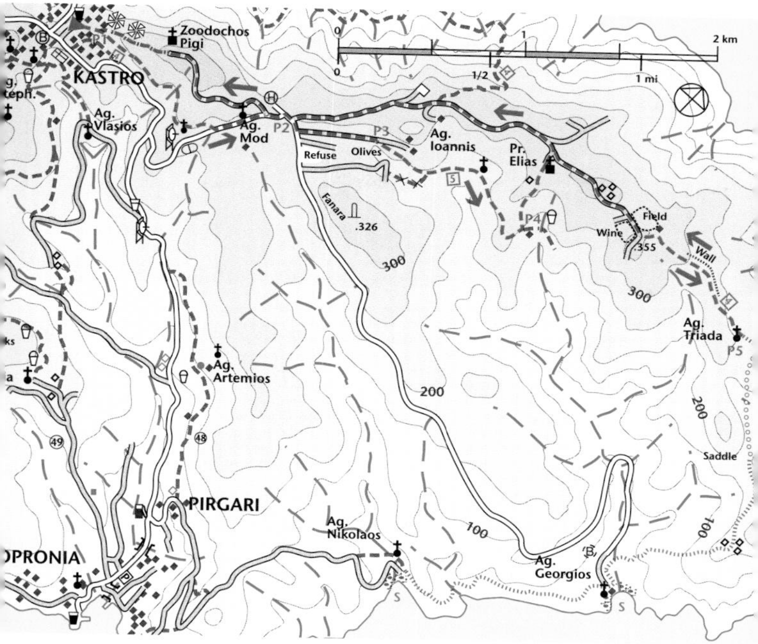

N36°42.121′/E25°08.248′) above an olive grove (right) ②.
Ahead of you lies a simply gorgeous, lonely trail above
terraced cornfields. You can pick out the Elias chapel on
1.00 the mountain. Down in the valley you later pass **St.
John's chapel** ③, from where the path takes a left sweep
round the mountain upon which the Elias chapel stands.
Now you should watch out: When descending, you see -
1.05 200m before the gully – a **small house** on the right below
the trail (**P4:** N36°42.198′/E25°08.858′). A few metres be-
!! fore actually reaching the house, you notice *indistinct
tracks* heading uphill to the left. Follow these, climbing to
the right of a dry wall. (If you are thirsty, stay longer on
the trail past the house and make for a well in the gully.)
At the end of the ascent you go past some ruins (left) be-
1.20 fore coming to the **Profítis Elias chapel.** The splendid
view rewards you for your efforts.

From there tracks lead over to a dirt track. In front of us
the Cycladic islands are laid out like a naval fleet. On the

★ left Mílos, then Antíparos, Páros, Náxos with the highest Cycladic peak, Zeus, to the right of it Iraklía and many more.

One really ought to delight in the regal spectacle a little longer before proceeding to the right along a roadway in the direction of "Malta". Later it runs, raised between
1.30 fields, through a **hollow.** In its extension it finally leads
1.45 you alongside a very long dry wall to **Agía Triáda Chapel** [4] (**P5:** N36°42.400'/E25°09.665').

> ***Alternative:*** The information board for hikers shows paths down to the very beautiful sandy beach of **Agios Geórgios.**
>
> The only drawback is that the paths depicted there hardly exist, which means that you have to hike without a path for a further two-and-a-half hours before reaching Aloprónia again along the coast.

2.10 The less strenuous option is to walk back to the **Elias chapel** and hoof down the roadway from there. Moving along above the steep coastline, you again command a view of the neighbouring islands, making you quite overlook the rubbish dump. Just before the latter a path marked "4" branches off to the right, but it is only recommended for hikers free from giddiness.

The roadway veers inland, once more passing the helipad. Immediately after that you take the **gravel track up to**
2.35 **the right** and come past the well-fortified rear of the de-
2.45 serted **fortified monastery of Zoodóchos Pigí**, perched mightily on the rock above the sea. Then skip down the
2.50 old steps leading to **Kástro**, along the decaying windmills.

Translation of special words for hikers

English	Français	Italiano	Nederlands	Svenska
boulder	bloc de rocher	masso	Rotsblok	klippblock
cairn	marquage	segnalato di pietre	Markeringssteen	vägmärke
cleft	fossé	fosso	Sloot	sänka
crest	crête	dorsale	Bergkam	bergskam
culvert	caniveau	passagio	water buis	vattenledning
defile	défilé	strada incassata	holleweg	hålväg
dirt road	chemin rural	sentiero di camp.	Onverharde weg	åkerväg
dip	dépression	depressione	Glooiing	sänka
ditch	fossé	fosso	Sloot	sänka
ford	gué	guado	doorwaadbare Pl.	vadställe
fork	bifurcation	bifurcazione	Wegsplitsing	vägskäl
furrow	fossé	fosso	Sloot	grav
gap	brèche	breccia	Bres	inskärning
clearing	clairière	radura	Open plek in bos	glänta
gorge	gorge	abisso	Kloof	ravin
gravel	pierraille	ghiaia	Steengruis	stenskärvor
grove	bosquet	bosco	Bosschage	lund
gully	cours d'eau	letto di fiume	Waterloop	vattendrag
heath	bruyère	brughiera	Heide	hed
hollow	dépression	depressione	Glooiing	sänka
incline	pente	pendio	Helling	sluttning
incision	fossé	fosso	Sloot	sänka
juniper	genévrier	ginepro	jeneverstruik	enbuske
past	près de	accanto a	naast	jämte
pebble	caillou	ciottolo	Kiezel	grus
pen	bergerie	stalla ovile	Stal	stall
ravine	ravin	abisso	Ravijn	ravin
rim	bords	orlo	Rand	kant
ridge	crête	cresta	Bergkam	bergskam
rubble	éboulis	ditriti	Steengruis	stenar
saddle	crête	sella	Bergrug	bergsrygg
schist	schiste	scisto	leisteen	skiffer
scree	éboulis	ditriti	Steengruis	stenar
scrub	fourré	sterpaglia	Doornbos	snår
slope	pente	pendio	Helling	sluttning
stream bed	lit	letto di fiume	Waterloop	vattendrag
strenuous	fatigant	faticoso	inspannend	ansträngande
trail	Pad	sentiero	Pad	stig
turn off	bifurcation	biforcazione	Afslag	avtagsväg
well	puits	pozzo	Bron	brunn

German version ISBN 978-3-9814047-8-4

Some Greek words for hikers:

Stress on the accents.

jássas	**hello**
ne	yes
óchi	no
parakaló	please
efcharistó	thank you
endáxi	okay
sto kaló	all the best
kalá	lovely
símera	today
ávrio	tomorrow
pósin óra?	How long?
pósso makriá ine ja?	How far is it to...?
puíne...?	Where is...?
óra	hour
neró	water
psomí	bread
tirí	cheese
míkro	small
mégalo	big
leoforió	bus
stásis	bus stop
enikáso	rent
aftókinito	auto
mechanáki	motor bike
podílato	bicycle
kaíki	boat
chora	**city**
chorio	hamlet
spíti	house
platía	square
parélia	harbour promenade
kástro	Venetian castle
pírgos	fortified Venetian castle
nekrotafío	cemetery
limáni	harbour
vrísi	fountain
stérna	cistern
kafenío	café, and how!
eklisiá	**church**
papás	priest
moní, monastíri	monastery
ksoklísi	chapel
panagía	Mother of God
panigíri	parish fair
ágios, agía, AG	saint
ikonostasio	icon altar screen
katholikón	central building in a monastery

kerós	weather
aéras	wind
meltémi	strong north wind
ílios	sun
wrochí	rain
omíchli	fog
níssos	island
farángi, langádi	ravine, gorge
kámpos, pláka	plains
livádi	meadow
déndro	tree
léfkes	poplars
dássos	forest
lófos	hill
wounó, óros	mountain
vígla	mountain peak
vráches	rock, cliff
spíleo	cave
thálassa	sea
órmos	bay
límni	lake
potámi	river
réma	dry bed
pigí	spring
pérazma	pass, ridge
xirolithía	dry wall
odiporió	**wandering**
isía	straight on
dexiá	right
aristerá	left
apáno	uphill
káto	downhill
kondá	near
makriá	far
ásfalto	asphalt street
drómos	street
chomaódromos	gravel street
dasikí odós	forest path
odós	path
skála	path of steps
monopáti	mule track
kalderími	paved way
katsikó drómos	goat path
yéfira	bridge
stavrodrómi	crossing, intersection
hártis	map
kutrúmbulo	path marking
phrygana	scrub, the island hiker's enemy

Abbreviations, Key

	hiking route on a road or dirt track
	hiking route on a street
- - - - -	hiking route on a path
....	hiking route without a path
ALT	alternative route, short-cut
← ⇐	walking direction / alternative
P	GPS point
	street
	dirt track, sandy track
MP	monopáti, mule track / marking
— — —	dry stream-bed (at times), hollow
	antenna
Ⓑ	bus stop / seasonal
P	parking area
Ⓗ	helicopter landing pad
	cemetery
+	wayside shrine, monument
	sports field
∩	cave
	medieval castle, dwelling tower / ruins
	ancient ruins, statue
▪ ▫	houses / ruins
	monastery, large church / ruins
	chapel / summit chapel / ruins
	taverna / open seasonally
	windmill/watermill, ruins
□ □	fountain, well, spring, reservoir, cistern
S	swimming possible

In the text:

!!	pay attention to turn-off!
	possible feelings of vertigo
OW	time for walking one way
★	the author's 20 favourite spots